Dec. 10/66

Happy Birthday

To Rachael and many

more.

From

Marilyn Horan

LIVE YOUR LIFE

LIVE YOUR LIFE

Maxims on the Fine Art of Living

By WALTER A. HEIBY

Harper & Row, Publishers
NEW YORK, EVANSTON, AND LONDON

 For information address Harper & Row, Publishers, Incorporated, 49 East 33rd Street, New York 16, N.Y.

FIRST EDITION

LIBRARY OF CONGRESS CATALOG CARD NUMBER: 66-25253

K-Q

To Eunice—queen of my kingdom,
my family—who, knowing intimately
the arts and the mathematics of love, daily lives
out one of its major axioms:

Marriage should be a 100–100 proposition.

ACKNOWLEDGMENTS

George Allen & Unwin, Ltd., London, England, for a quotation from *For People Under Pressure* by David H. Fink, copyright © 1956 by David H. Fink. For a quotation from *Tradition and Progress* by Gilbert Murray, copyright 1922 by George Allen & Unwin, Ltd. For quotations from *Analysis of Matter* by Bertrand Russell, copyright 1927 by George Allen & Unwin, Ltd.

American Physical Society for a quotation from an article by Michael Polanyi which appeared in *Review of Modern Physics*, copyright © 1962 by the American Physical Society.

A. S. Barnes & Company, Inc., for a quotation from *Ex Libris Carissimis* by Christopher Morley, copyright 1932 by Christopher Morley.

Beacon Press for a quotation from *Today's Children and Yesterday's Heritage* by Sophia L. Fahs, copyright 1952 by Beacon Press.

Bobbs-Merrill Co. for a quotation from *The Will Rogers Book* by Paula M. Love, copyright © 1961 by Paula M. Love.

Cadillac Motor Car Company for an article from an advertisement in *The Saturday Evening Post*, January 2, 1915, copyright by Cadillac Motor Car Co.

Doubleday & Company, Inc., for a quotation from *Just So Stories* by Rudyard Kipling, copyright 1902 by Rudyard Kipling.

Dover Publications, Inc., for quotations from *Analysis of Matter* by Bertrand Russell, copyright 1954 by Dover Publications, Inc.

Melvin J. Evans Company for a quotation from *It Works* by Melvin J. Evans, published by Democracy in Action Foundation (Human Development in Action Foundation), copyright © 1965 by Melvin J. Evans.

B. C. Forbes Publishing Co., Inc., for a quotation from *The Silver Lining* by Thomas Dreier, copyright 1923 by B. C. Forbes Publishing Co.

Harper & Row, Publishers, Inc., for a quotation from *Edison, His Life and Inventions* by Dyer, Martin and Meadowcroft, copyright 1929 by Harper & Row, Publishers, Inc. For a quotation from *On Being a Real Person* by Harry Emerson Fosdick, copyright 1943 by Harper & Row, Publishers, Inc. For quotations from *The Art of Loving* by Erich Fromm, copyright © 1956 by Erich Fromm. For quotations from *The Choice to Love* by Robert Raynolds, copyright © 1959 by Robert Raynolds. For a quotation from *In Praise of Gratitude* by Robert Raynolds, copyright © 1961 by Robert Raynolds.

Houghton Mifflin Company for a quotation from *On the Contrary* by Sydney J. Harris, copyright © 1964 by Sydney J. Harris.

Macmillan & Company Ltd. for a quotation from *Just So Stories* by Rudyard Kipling, copyright 1902 by Rudyard Kipling.

Nightingale-Conant Corp. for quotations from the Earl Nightingale Radio Program "Our Changing World," copyright © 1960 by Earl Nightingale.

Prentice-Hall, Inc., for a quotation from *How to Live with Yourself* by Murray Banks, copyright 1951 by Murray Banks. For a quotation from *The Art and Skill of Getting Along with People* by Sylvanus M. Duvall, copyright

© 1961 by Prentice-Hall, Inc. For a quotation from *The Will to Live* by Arnold A. Hutschnecker, copyright 1951 by Arnold A. Hutschnecker. For a quotation from *The Secrets of Selling Yourself to People* by James T. Mangan, copyright © 1961 by Prentice-Hall, Inc. For a quotation from *The Human Side of Successful Communication* by Robert E. Moore, copyright © 1961 by Prentice-Hall, Inc. For a quotation from *The Success System That Never Fails* by W. Clement Stone, copyright © 1962 by Prentice-Hall, Inc.

Random House, Inc., for a quotation from *Gift from the Sea* by Anne Morrow Lindbergh, copyright © 1955 by Anne Morrow Lindbergh.

Fleming H. Revell Co. for a quotation from *Better Church Bulletins* by Stella Barnett, copyright © 1955 by Fleming H. Revell Co.

The Seabury Press, Inc., for quotations from *Christian Living* by Stephen F. Bayne, Jr., copyright © 1957 by the Seabury Press, Inc.

Simon & Schuster, Inc., for a quotation from *How to Win Friends and Influence People* by Dale Carnegie, copyright 1936 by Dale Carnegie. For a quotation from *For People Under Pressure* by David H. Fink, copyright © 1956 by David H. Fink. For a quotation by Charles H. Percy from *This I Believe* edited by Edward R. Murrow, copyright 1954 by Help, Inc.

Stein and Day for quotations from *Advice from a Failure* by Jo Coudert, copyright © 1965 by Jo Coudert.

A. P. Watt & Son, London, England, for a quotation from *Just So Stories* by Rudyard Kipling, copyright 1902 by Rudyard Kipling.

The World's Work (1913), London, England, for a quotation from *How to Win Friends and Influence People* by Dale Carnegie, copyright 1938 by Dale Carnegie.

Acknowledgment is made to Mrs. George Bambridge for a quotation from *Just So Stories* by Rudyard Kipling. To Russell B. Field for a quotation by Charles Kellogg Field. To Judge Jonah Goldstein for a quotation from the bronze in the lobby of the Grand Street Boys' Clubhouse. To Mrs. Lou Lockhart for a quotation by Eugene L'Hote. To Virgil Markham for a quotation by Edwin Markham. To Hugh Noyes for a quotation by Alfred Noyes. To the *Saturday Review* for a quotation by Norman Cousins.

Acknowledgment is also made to Clyde Bedell, Archibald MacLeish, Rosa Zagnoni Marinoni and to Michael Polanyi for permission to use some of their material.

Contents

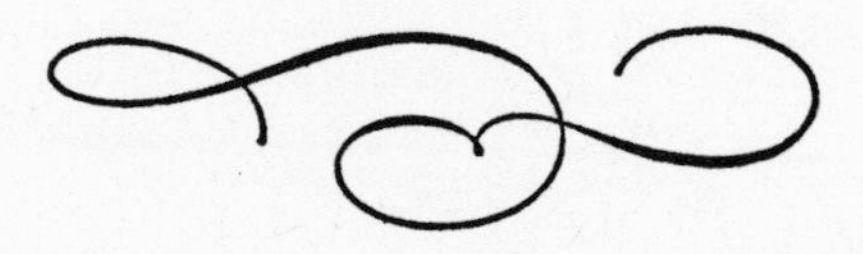

May you live all the days
of your life.

—JONATHAN SWIFT

Preface

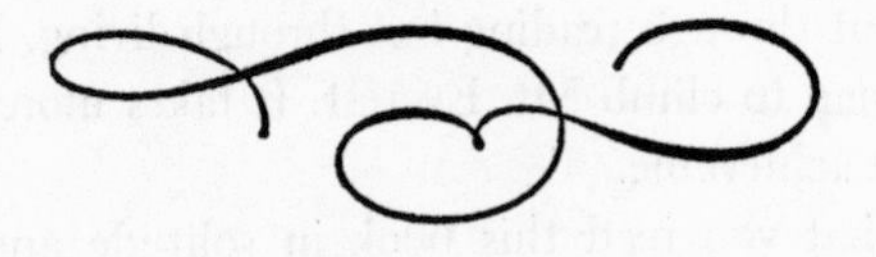

The proper study of mankind is man.
—ALEXANDER POPE

Here's to life . . . and to our *living* of it!

This book began with an unusual, narrow, and personal purpose—to instruct Walter Heiby. As I thought of ideas and rules of conduct to aid me in living a fuller, richer, more friendly and useful life I jotted them down. Now that the collection has grown into this book, I invite you to consider these thoughts with me.

These are thoughts and action ideas that I feel compelled to review frequently. Many of these principles, most of which have certainly occurred to millions since the time men first took their families to live in caves, have been set down in various forms by Jesus, Confucius, Benjamin Franklin, Ralph Waldo Emerson, William James and others. I have not "learned" these rules in any degree beyond the student's definition of "learn." Perhaps great truths are never really learned; they must be learned and lived, then relearned and relived. We must come to appreciate that "learning" is best defined as "living." To understand human nature we must study not just books but men, their actions and their words, *our* actions and *our* words. Goodness can be acquired only through the practice of being good, friendliness only through being friendly, helpfulness only through being helpful. We learn to live in a loving way by exercising our capacity to love. We learn to live happy lives not through reading but through living. It takes more than a trail map to climb Mt. Everest. It takes more than a book to achieve the achievable.

I suggest that you read this book in solitude and only a few thoughts per sitting. It should take you several months to read. To read the book more rapidly will lessen whatever effect for good it may hold for you. While you are reading and digesting it, you may wish to mark your place and turn ahead or turn back to other chapters for help in solving an immediate problem or in facing a special situation. Do so, but let me urge you again not to attempt a fast run-through, for that will only serve to make the book powerless to help you in any way. And unless you have borrowed the book from the library or from a friend, read it with pencil in hand. Write in the margins your agreement or disagreement with what you read, underline passages for future review, mark any items you may wish to reread. A book becomes valuable to you when it ceases to be just the author's and becomes *yours*.

Each of our lives is, to a large degree, what our mothers and fathers made it—through the gift of love and through the gift of discipline. I thank my parents, Laura and Albert Heiby, for the love they gave me and for their discipline, controlled and determined by love. This vital love-discipline ratio that you and I control will determine to a great extent, the happiness, the sensitivity to beauty, the will-to-action, the success, the contentment with which our children live their lives.

Most of us know what we must do to live a happy, useful life—but our memories are poor and we can use some reminding. As

Goethe said, "Everything has been thought of before, but the difficulty is to think of it again." The purpose of *Live Your Life* is to remind. To be happier and to live more meaningful lives we must not merely read; we must live at least some of the thoughts of this book. Making friends and living a happy life hinges not on the theory but on the act of giving others our love, our enthusiasm, our help, our sympathy, our interest, our encouragement. As we read and live the thoughts expressed here we will be making promises to ourselves. Above all other such promises let's promise ourselves that we'll keep those that we make to ourselves.

Someday the world will come to the realization that the most important thing in life is amicable, cooperative relations among people and among nations. Then the primary purpose of our schools will be to teach pupils how to get along with themselves and with others. When the world's millions know their lessons well, there will be no more crime and there will be perpetual peace.

Through the centuries men have been slowly developing a stronger feeling of humanity toward one another. Certainly one of the major forces shaping the evolution of man is altruism. Perhaps in another thousand centuries men will no longer display an urgent dedication toward furthering just their own interests but rather exhibit an intense devotion to the interests of others.

I wish to thank the authors, publishers and other copyright owners who have given permission for their material to be reprinted in this book. I am deeply grateful to my wife, Eunice, to my father, Albert H. Heiby, and to Harold E. Grove for help in editing. I thank my mother, Laura Heiby, and my father for establishing a home based on love and one in which many of my present attitudes, as reflected by my writings, were formed when I was very young. My gratitude also goes to my sister, Myrtle G. Shaw, whose love and encouragement have been important in forming my views of life. My thankful appreciation is also due my good friend Howard L. Taylor, with whom I have discussed the pleasures and problems of life on countless occasions since we met in grammar school some time before we each had reached the worldly-wise age of ten. My love and appreciation go to my children, Pamela and Ronald, who, along with their mother, have added so much joy and happiness to my own life and who have had, therefore, a great influence on me. I also thank my loyal typist, Gertrude Ramelow, who laboriously prepared the manuscript for publication.

I thank you, too, the reader, for devoting the time to share these thoughts with me. May this book become not just a part of your library but a part of your life.

—Walter A. Heiby

May, 1966

LIVE YOUR LIFE

1

The Enjoyment of Living

Never forget that happiness is like a butterfly. The more you chase it and chase it directly–*the more it will always just elude you. But if you sit down quietly and turn your attention to other things, then it comes and softly sits on your shoulder!*

—DR. MURRAY BANKS

Yesterday is but a dream,
Tomorrow is only a vision.
But today well lived makes
Every yesterday a dream of happiness,
And every tomorrow a vision of hope.
Look well, therefore, to this day.

—KALIDASA

The grand essentials to happiness in this life are something to do, something to love, and something to hope for.

—JOSEPH ADDISON

(2) *Live Your Life*

Happiness, I have discovered, is nearly always a rebound from hard work. It is one of the follies of men to imagine that they can enjoy mere thought, or emotion, or sentiment. As well try to eat beauty! For happiness must be tricked! She loves to see men at work. She loves sweat, weariness, self-sacrifice. She will be found not in palaces but lurking in cornfields and factories and hovering over littered desks; she crowns the unconscious head of the busy child. If you look up suddenly from hard work you will see her, but if you look too long she fades sorrowfully away.

—David Grayson

Before we set our hearts too much upon anything, let us examine how happy they are who already possess it.

—François de la Rochefoucauld

The kingdom of God is within you.

—Jesus (Luke 17:21)

Happiness is a perfume you cannot pour on others without getting a few drops on yourself.

—Ralph Waldo Emerson

It is something to be able to paint a particular picture, or to carve a statue, and so to make a few objects beautiful; but it is far more glorious to carve and paint the very atmosphere and medium through which we look. . . . To affect the quality of the day—that is the highest of arts.

—Henry David Thoreau

When I bought my farm, I did not know what a bargain I had in the bluebirds, bobolinks, and thrushes; as little did I know what sublime mornings and sunsets I was buying.

—Ralph Waldo Emerson

Gratitude is the memory of the heart; therefore forget not to say often, I have all I have ever enjoyed.

—Lydia M. Child

(3) The Enjoyment of Living

Happiness is the only product in the world that multiplies by division.

—Judge Jonah Goldstein

The true riches of life are hidden in the hearts and minds of men.

—W. Clement Stone

Most people are about as happy as they make up their minds to be.

—Abraham Lincoln

Much more happiness is to be found in the world than gloomy eyes discover.

—Friedrich Wilhelm Nietzsche

It is better to desire things we have than have the things we desire.

—Henry Van Dyke

Do not mistake what your lifework is; it is your life.

—Jo Coudert

The meaning of life is to live it!

There are two forms of wisdom. One wisdom relates to facts—the other relates to living. The wisdom of facts produces ideas and relationships which are valuable in science, in business, in art, in literature. The wisdom of living finds happiness in life and discovers ways of bringing it to others.

Enjoy as many of your daily tasks as you can. Do the others and enjoy having them behind you.

❧❧

You are not likely to find the flowers of happiness around the corner if you fail to see those now at your feet.

❧❧

A source of unhappiness, or failure to achieve full happiness, is the habit of invidious comparison. To one who constantly compares, there was once a pie more delicious than this one, a day that was sunnier, a profit that was greater, a girl who was prettier, a climate elsewhere that seemed more favorable. The act of comparison should be restricted to the arts, to scientific analyses, to other fields employing quantitative relationships and to phenomena where people are not involved. Comparison that involves people and their acts and those circumstances intimately connected with our happiness must be purged from our thinking. Happiness is achieved through enjoyment of the present situation undiluted by thoughts of similar circumstances that appear more favorable when viewed in retrospect.

❧❧

There is a vast difference between happiness and pleasure. Pleasure is a false face that is more often the mask of discontent than of happiness.

❧❧

Let's talk about our happiness. By telling others how happy we are, we will discover that we *are* very happy. We'll also help our listeners to think happy thoughts. The happiness we induce in others induces, in turn, greater happiness in ourselves.

❧❧

The man who has found something he can be enthusiastic about has found a fountainhead of happiness.

❧❧

The happy person through his friendliness—his appreciation—his smiles—continually puts happiness back in circulation.

❧❧

There is beauty in the sunshine; there is beauty in the rain. That beauty is there which we ourselves have brought to the sunshine and to the rain.

❧❧

Happiness exists where there is, in addition to the things that bring satisfaction and contentment, a conscious awareness that one has these things. Most of us have the first qualification for happiness—we have an abundance of blessings. It is in the second area that we fall short: we fail to recognize the fact that we have all these things. Through such recognition we achieve happiness.

❧❧

When this moment is gone will I look back and say, "How happy I was then!"

❧❧

All of us have the capacity to manufacture trouble anywhere, any time, out of anything or out of nothing. Happy persons *decline* to use this ability.

❧❧

Here is a universal characteristic of happy, successful people I can easily assume. I will tell others what is *right* about people; I will keep to myself what I think is wrong.

❧❧

Not what we have or are or do, but our attitude toward what we have and are and do, is what makes us happy or unhappy.

❧❧

If we would change our lives we must first change our attitudes. Happiness is not created by what happens to us but by our attitude toward each happening.

❧❧

Welcome your problems. Through solving problems we gain life's greatest satisfactions.

❧❧

If someone says, "Gee, it's a hot day," we might reply, "It would be nice to have some of this weather five or six months from now, wouldn't it?" If another says, "It's terribly foggy," we might reply, "We're in the clouds!"

Let's resolve never again to initiate a complaint about the weather. Such complaints merely increase our own discomfort and add to the misery of others. Silence is more acceptable as conversation than words that produce unhappiness.

❧❧

We are posing an unrewarding question if we ask ourselves, "What am I getting out of my marriage—my religion—my job?" Ask instead, "What am I giving to my marriage—my religion—my job?" Instead of thinking, "What can I get?" why not think, "What can I give?" It is the attitude of *giving* that leads to a full life.

❦

The measure of our happiness is the gifts of ourselves which we give to others.

❦

Most of our days are spent in helping others. Husbands and fathers going to work each day, whether they feel like it or not, facing problems, worries, and discouragements, are living lives of service to their wives and children. Wives and mothers, doing the thousands of household chores in their twenty-four-hour workday, are living lives of service to their husbands and children. Every business, every profession is based on service to others; every employee of every business is serving constantly and making worthwhile contributions to society. You and I are living lives of service. So let's feel good about it!

❦

The most important thing in our lives is what we are doing *now*—whether it be eating a grape or doing research that may bring a Nobel Prize.

❦

Whenever I think of it I am going to put the start of a smile on my face—not a full smile but just its imperceptible start. With the slightest encouragement I will let it grow into a full smile.

❦

Trusting others, even though that trust may occasionally be violated, leads to more happiness than results from living a life of doubt and distrust.

❧

Each time I visit a restaurant I will try to find at least one food to compliment. I'll praise it as highly as I honestly can to the waitress and ask her to pass on the compliment to the chef. The more happiness we give away to others the more we have left for ourselves.

❧

Happiness is the by-product of striving to attain worthwhile goals.

❧

Here's an answer to boredom and unhappiness: find a way to help someone.

❧

A smile delights at least two—the giver and the receiver. A smile is the great enemy of anger, despair, hopelessness, discouragement.

Let's think of persons we particularly like or persons who are especially popular. Don't most of these men and women have one trait in common—pleasant, frequent smiles and eager, outgoing expressions?

❧

Live life to the fullest! Everything around us—the song of birds, a blade of grass, the sunset, the oil gauges in our cars, a drill press drilling holes, the letters and the orders that will arrive today, the customers we will meet, the men we will pass on the street and never get to know—all these are interesting and exciting. Don't continually look on happiness as something that will happen only in the future—next Sunday or next Christmas or when we retire, or during next summer's vacation. Happiness must not be thought of as a distant goal. Unless we can learn to be happy this very minute we will probably never be happy.

❦❦

Realize the truth in William James's reversal of cause and effect: "We are happy because we smile." Each morning begin your day with smiles given to the bathroom mirror. Continue your day with smiles for friends and for strangers as you pass them on the street. You will be happy if you smile.

❦❦

Let's not concern ourselves so completely with yesterday's regrets or with tomorrow's fateful possibilities that we fail to fulfill the promises of today. Start each morning determined to make the most of today. The past cannot be more favorably re-enacted by our dwelling upon it. The future's varied calamities that we continually envision, virtually never come to pass. Live *today!*

❦❦

Your ulcer can't grow while you're laughing.

❦❦

Having more material *things* does not produce happiness. Happiness comes through striving to get the most out of what we already have.

❦❦

In matters of happiness cultivate a good memory; in matters of sadness, a good forgettery.

❦

The sunset does not give us the gift of beauty. We bring the beauty to the sunset. In bringing the gift of a happy smile to others, we help give ourselves happiness.

❦

Happiness is a by-product of the search for enough time to complete one's projects. Unhappiness accompanies the search for projects to take up the time.

❦

Happiness is determined, to a large extent, by the degree to which we give love and accept love.

❦

Happiness is less an effect than it is a cause. Cheerful persons expect good things to happen, expect to be successful, expect to enjoy themselves. The happy person experiences tragedies and has his problems just as unhappy persons do, but he gets over his difficulties more rapidly and once again finds that the world is a wonderful place and that life is good. A positive attitude *causes* good things to happen.

❦

Happiness isn't found in searching for it. It comes quietly while we are helping others.

❦

Every man, woman, and child on this earth has an overwhelming desire to be loved, to be wanted, to be appreciated. To the extent that we can fulfill this desire will we give happiness and find happiness ourselves.

❧❧

When we praise or compliment someone, we give pleasure not only to the one we praise but to ourselves.

❧❧

A man's contentment lies in enthusiastic appreciation for the things he has; a man's misery lies in excessive desire for the things he has not.

❧❧

No man is rich if his money has cost him too much happiness, love, or peace of mind. Let's not pay too much happiness for our money.

❧❧

Unless we find beauty and happiness in our back yard we will never find them in the mountains.

2

Control of Fear and Worry

A molehill man is a pseudo-busy manager who comes to work at 9 A.M. and finds a molehill on his desk. He has until 5 P.M. to make this molehill into a mountain. An accomplished molehill man will often have his mountain finished before lunch.

—FRED ALLEN

Keep your face to the sun and the shadows will fall behind.

—UNKNOWN

If Winter comes, can Spring be far behind?

—PERCY BYSSHE SHELLEY

When you have a lemon, make a lemonade.

—UNKNOWN

The North wind made the Vikings.

—SCANDINAVIAN SAYING

(13) *Control of Fear and Worry*

Because you have occasional low spells of despondence, don't despair. The sun has a sinking spell every night, but it rises again all right the next morning.

—Henry van Dyke

It takes rough seas to make good sailors and great captains.

—Unknown

To dare is great. To bear is greater. Bravery we share with brutes. Fortitude with saints.

—Charles Force Deems

Never let yesterday use up too much of today.

—Will Rogers

Fear is finally put in its proper place only in those persons who, even when they are afraid, feel that whether they are afraid or not is a minor matter.

—Harry Emerson Fosdick

If all our misfortunes were laid in one common heap, whence everyone must take an equal portion, most people would be content to take their own and depart.

—Socrates

Common sense does not ask an impossible chessboard, but it takes the one before it and plays the game.

—Wendell Phillips

In two words: Im Possible!

—Samuel Goldwyn

Worry never robs tomorrow of its sorrow, but only saps today of its strength.

—A. J. Cronin

Don't worry about worry! Worry, when it is constructive deliberation concerning situations over which we have some control, is a perfectly normal function of a mind striving to find the solution to a problem. As such it is better referred to as *meditation.* Only when it is under the influence of negative thinking does it become the evil called *anxiety.* Harmful worry is the worry that is *anxiety;* productive worry is the worry that is *meditation.*

Worry is a spring shower. The rainbow and flowers will follow.

A powerful technique for combating worry is to devote our energies to gathering facts about the problem that is causing us to worry. Let's begin by writing down on a piece of paper just what it is that we are worrying about. Then gather the facts about our problem in as disinterested, impartial a manner as possible, recording in one list facts that work against us and, in a separate list, those that are in our favor. After the facts are written down it is generally far easier to interpret them and arrive at a decision. Once that decision has been reached and we begin to act on it, worry will disappear.

When we put off 'til tomorrow what we could just as well do today and continue to worry about the undone task, we are wasting energy. When we have an unpleasant or difficult assignment we should do it immediately unless through delay we may acquire

first time. Fear is the mind's reaction to the new, the unknown. Fear is normal. Fear is not to be feared.

What is the formula for overcoming shyness and self-consciousness? Simply this: *Forget yourself. Think of something else.* If you are speaking before a group, think about your subject. Forget about what your listeners may think of your speaking ability and concentrate instead on giving them your message. Think, instead, of how your message can help your listeners.

Shyness and self-consciousness are by-products of too much thinking about ourselves. They cannot exist when our minds are filled with thoughts of helping others.

Trouble develops in us the ability to meet it. It strengthens and matures those it touches. Trouble frequently finds for us our dearest friends. *We need the night to see the stars!*

Do we dread discussing a problem with the boss? Talk it over and worry disappears. Postpone action and fear increases. Are we afraid to make a certain phone call? Make it and be relieved. Delay the call, and our timidity increases. *Action conquers fear and worry.*

To worry is perfectly normal. In fact, if someone were completely devoid of worry in a threatening situation we would rightly question his sanity. However, let's worry about really threatening situations, not about improbable remote possibilities that virtually never occur. We ought to define worry as "a search for a problem's solution" and realize that not only is such worry normal but it is desirable because if we do enough of it we will have solved our problem.

❦❦

What is your greatest enemy and what is mine? Fear!

❦❦

To successfully defeat fear we must first face the fact of its existence. Fear is not defeated through denial but through recognition. Let's face our fear and subject it to analysis in order to determine its cause. If we find that our fear serves a function in promoting our survival, we should respect it. If it does not serve such a function, laugh it out of existence!

❦❦

When we start a new, more difficult job we should realize that not only we, but everyone beginning a new job, suffers from a fear of inadequacy. This fear is not only normal but is actually a good indication—an indication that we are intelligent enough to be on guard against errors.

No person was ever really prepared to accept a more responsible job. The man who is truly prepared for his job has accepted a position that is unworthy of his talents. Let's tackle the new job unafraid. We can do it—and do it well!

❦❦

Worry is the overevaluation of the probability of the possible. I've dreamed up many troubles—but lived out very few.

❦❦

How can we overcome our shyness, embarrassment, and self-consciousness? A useful three-step technique is to:

1. Take a piece of paper and write on it the reasons for our shyness, embarrassment, and self-consciousness.
2. Opposite each reason write a more factual, optimistic analysis of the situation.
3. Keep repeating the optimistic evaluations whenever we face this particular embarrassing situation.

How do we apply this technique to overcome our shyness, embarrassment, and self-consciousness when we are called upon to speak before a group? At the left we write the reasons for our shyness and at the right the more optimistic evaluation of the facts:

Reasons for Shyness	*Optimistic Evaluation*
A. Speaking to a group is a fearful predicament.	A. Speaking to a group involves no threat to me in any way. Each day thousands survive this situation.
B. My audience will dislike me.	B. People, in general, like other people and will like me.
C. I will look stupid to my audience.	C. I am speaking about a subject which I understand better than those in my audience.
D. I am tense and nervous before an audience.	D. A certain amount of tenseness is experienced by all speakers and is perfectly normal. I have lived through similarly tense situations before and will survive this one also.

Repeating this list of optimistic evaluations next time we must face an audience should greatly alleviate our shyness, embarrassment, and self-consciousness.

❧❧

What is the formula for avoiding fear? Become so completely absorbed in what you are doing that there is no time for fear or worry.

❧❧

Worry gives us more pain than the thing or event about which we worry.

❧❧

We must learn to fear the actual rather than the merely possible.

❧❧

If we think less of the impression we are making on others and more about how much we like them, we will have no time to feel shy or inferior. Feelings of inferiority and shyness become nonexistent for those who think continually of helping others to solve *their* problems.

❧❧

Never forget that it is completely normal to feel excitement—get butterflies in the stomach—when we meet others for the first time or when we give a speech. We become increasingly nervous when we forget this fundamental fact of human relations. Our nervousness is kept under control when we realize that apprehension in meeting others and in giving a speech is felt by everyone, including prominent persons whom we admire for their poise.

When speaking in public let's concentrate on getting our message across. The jitters will be gone by the time we have reached the end of our first sentence.

❧❧

Divide your problems into two categories: those over which you have control and those you can do nothing about. Concentrate your energies toward solving solvable problems. Do not worry about problems over which you have no control.

❧❧

Logical fears have what sociologists term "survival value"—they aid men in their attempt to stay alive. The man who fears to drive his car at 100 miles per hour has a logical fear—a fear that increases the probability of survival of himself and of others.

Logical fears are valuable. Phobias, on the other hand, are illogical fears—those that have no survival value. A phobia may involve fear of any of hundreds of things, such as these:

great heights	death	animals
open places	darkness	stairs
lightning	crowds	insects
empty rooms	snakes	sharp objects
enclosed places	drugs	loss of money
dirt	noise	sex
bacteria	bodies of water	

Many of the above things may at times be objects of logical fears. The girl who is afraid to walk down a dark street in a neighborhood known for the holdups and assaults that have taken place there has a logical fear. She should not try to dispel this fear; she should be guided by it and travel out of her way to avoid that dark street.

When we are afraid let's analyze to see if our fear is logical or not. It may be a logical fear that has real survival value or it may be a phobia.

A phobia which many of us have is Xenophobia, the fear of meeting strangers. Cro-Magnon man's fear of the noise outside his cave was a logical fear. It might have been a bear which had to be fought off with spears, rocks, and knives or it might have been a stranger who had come to steal his wife. But our fear or shyness in meeting strangers has, in the vast majority of instances, no survival value. This man we are about to meet is a friendly human being, or, if he does not seem to be friendly, it may be because he is too shy to show friendliness. If he is too shy to show his friendliness he is in desperate need of our smiles and kind words.

❧❧

The greatest hero is he who, trembling, does the thing he fears to do!

❧❧

Here is a way we can dispel worry. Ask ourselves what is the probability that the dire event we are worrying about will occur. If the probability is near zero, we should stop worrying! Let's just tell ourselves, "The law of averages says this won't happen."

❧❧

Each time that fear is met head-on and is conquered one gains strength to meet the adversary again.

❧❧

To lose our shyness and self-consciousness we must come to realize that when we enter a room full of people all eyes are *not* turned upon us. People are too interested in themselves to be overly concerned about us. They are *not* thinking about us and are *not* watching every move we make.

To lose our shyness we must concentrate on, and recognize the importance of, what others are doing and thinking. Let's realize, too, that others—those who appear to be so self-reliant—may also suffer from self-consciousness. Realizing this, we ought to concentrate our efforts on helping others to feel at home, to help others overcome *their* shyness. In helping others, we help ourselves.

❧❧

An important cause of shyness in talking with others, or of stage fright when speaking before a group, is our overconcern with the impression we are making. Instead, concentrate on getting the idea across and on its value to your listeners. A sincere desire to help, instruct, or entertain others will reduce shyness and tensions.

❧❧

Here's a way of coping with today's worry about some future event:

Assume that the absolute worst will happen. But how bad is that? Will we end up in jail? Will we lose our job? Will we lose a thousand dollars? Will our business fail? Just how bad is the worst that can happen?

Next let's resign ourselves to the acceptance of this worst possible occurrence. Realize that even this dire possibility isn't so bad. When we do this we should note a feeling of relaxation since the future's uncertainty has been replaced, in our minds, by an acceptance of the worst possible eventuality.

Finally, we should work continually to improve upon this worst possible occurrence. Our progress will be good because the relaxed attitude brought on by our acceptance of the worst will help greatly to improve the situation.

❧❧

When you have worries, don't keep silent while the tension mounts. Talk out the problem with your wife, your husband, a friend, a doctor, a clergyman. Talking helps clarify the problem, frequently results in new ideas for meeting the difficulty, relieves tension and generally leads to a decision as to what must be done.

❧❧

The cause of shyness lies in too much consciousness of self. If we will look upon every person with a sincere desire to learn about his ideas, his vocation, and his hobbies, we will lose our shyness. We will be too busy thinking of him to be concerned with ourselves. When we are thinking of others, we can't be shy.

❧❧

A year from now you and I are not going to be worrying about this problem that seems so tremendous today. Why should we worry about it today? Let's try to view today's problem from the viewpoint we'll have next year.

❧❧

Pick up any history book—one treating of the days of ancient Rome, or of Europe in the Middle Ages, or of America in pioneer days or of any other phase of history. Regardless of which period of the world's history we read about, we will find that poverty, intolerance, crime, famine, and disease were far greater problems in that period than they are now. Since these conditions have greatly improved, shouldn't we be optimistic about the possibility of eliminating even the age-old problem of war?

❧❧

To combat difficulty in falling asleep because of continual worrying about problems, get a pencil and paper and write down all those problems for consideration in the morning. Making a record of the problems will help free the mind and induce relaxation.

❧❧

To lose your fear, act as if you're not afraid!

❧❧

If you worried about what others think of you no more often than they actually think about you, you'd do very little worrying.

❦

Promote peace of mind by always allowing an extra fifteen minutes to get to any scheduled meeting, to keep an appointment, or to catch a train. It will be minutes well invested toward elimination of health-destroying tension. Energy that might have been dissipated in nervousness will be conserved for more efficient performance of the work at hand. Have a book in your pocket to read during the fifteen minutes.

❦

Excessive concern for physical health can undermine mental health. Fear of a disease can cause more harm than the disease itself.

❦

When we discover that we have an illogical fear, let's define our fear using just one or two words. Examples might be fear of *high places* or of *meeting strangers*.

Then let's write on a piece of paper the words we associate with our fear. If we have a fear of *high places* or of *meeting strangers*, our respective lists might be these:

For High Places	For Meeting Strangers
dizzy	stares
terrifying	unsure
dangerous	tongue-tied
	blunder
	unfriendly
	mistakes
	terrifying
	tense

Next step in our attempt to get rid of our phobia is to make a list of opposite *positive* words and place them adjacent to the negative words we have already listed. These positive words need not be antonyms but should simply represent our own opposite impressions. Such lists of positive words which we write adjacent to the negative words might be

FOR HIGH PLACES

Negative list	*Positive list*
dizzy	awe inspiring
terrifying	exciting
dangerous	safe

FOR MEETING STRANGERS

Negative list	*Positive list*
stares	smiles
unsure	confident
tongue-tied	fluent
blunder	competent
unfriendly	friendly
mistakes	correct
terrifying	exciting
tense	relaxed

Once these lists are developed, they are to be used thereafter whenever we experience our phobia. First we read the negative word list aloud and in a tone of voice that shows the unpleasantness we feel. Then let's read the list of positive words with a tone of voice that indicates the pleasantness of the ideas represented by that list. Finally, repeat the reading of the pleasant list again and perhaps a third or fourth time.

Whenever we need help with our phobia, we read the negative

word list and then read the positive word list two or three or more times. We always end up with the reading of the positive list. In time our phobia will disappear, and readings will no longer be needed.

❦❦

Worry can't enter a mind that's busy with other matters.

❦❦

When you have a fear, admit that you are afraid, but realize that fear is the normal way of reacting to any unknown situation. The fears we do not admit having do the most harm. When we admit the fear, we have taken a big step toward effecting its elimination.

Next write down the reasons for the fear. Then study the reasons on this list, one by one, to determine their validity. Chances are we will find that reason after reason is invalid. Once we have eliminated all the reasons, we will no longer have that fear.

❦❦

Decisions are difficult to make when insufficient facts are known. Instead of worrying, let's search out the facts. A plentiful supply of facts relating to a problem makes worry unnecessary for the nature of the decision that must be made usually becomes obvious. Decision spells the death of worry.

❦❦

Today is the tomorrow over which I needlessly worried yesterday. Today's tomorrow will be as fine as yesterday's.

❦❦

Once a decision is made, let's not waste time and effort in constantly reviewing it, but spend our energies instead in carrying it out.

❧❧

The way to a tension-free life is to find an increasing number of things we can tolerate and fewer things we feel compelled to fight against.

❧❧

The tensions of a man are not caused by events but by his attitude toward those events. Many events are more disastrous in a man's opinion than they are in fact.

❧❧

Do your worrying before the race, while you are studying the racing form, not after your bet is placed and the horses are coming down the stretch.

❧❧

Our most difficult problems, masked by related fears, exist in the realm of the imagination. Problems faced realistically become less formidable, then solvable, and then cease to exist. The only remnant of the problem is the pride of having met and solved it.

❧❧

Fear spreads like a contagious disease from one person to another. In attempting to help those suffering from the disease of fear, be careful that you too do not become its victim.

❧❧

The worth of a decision is often proportional to the courage needed to make it.

❧❧

The brave man is afraid but conquers his fear.

❦

Problems seem so difficult; solutions, when found, so obvious.

❦

Patience and the passage of time solve all problems, cure all troubles, dissipate all worries.

❦

A problem is a chrysalis that awaits its butterfly. When its time has come, the solution will emerge. Never believe the chrysalis will fail in its destiny. Never believe a problem will remain, for long, unsolved.

3

Building Confidence and Enthusiasm

The happiest people on earth are those who are emotionally involved in what they're doing. This calm cool collected bit is all right for cows, camels and turtles, but it will never produce a great sermon, symphony, play, business, piece of architecture, painting, marriage or the miracle of a child.

—Earl Nightingale

Are not minimum hours and maximum wages contraceptives against the freedom of love in our work?

—Robert Raynolds

When love and skill work together . . . expect a masterpiece.

—John Ruskin

I never did a days' work in my life. It was all fun.

—Thomas Edison

The great aim of education is not knowledge but action.

—Herbert Spencer

The mintage of wisdom is to know that rest is rust, and that real life is in love, laughter and work.

—Elbert Hubbard

Creative experience simply cannot be equated in terms of dollars. When I work in the garden I'm having fun. How can I pay a gardener a dollar an hour to have fun for me? The landscaping that results is simply an extra dividend.

—Dr. David H. Fink

If a man does only what is required of him, he is a slave. The moment he does more, he is a free man.

—Unknown

Nothing is really work unless you would rather be doing something else.

—Sir James M. Barrie

What I admire in Columbus is not his having discovered a world, but his having gone to search for it on the faith of an opinion.

—A. Robert Jacques Turgot

Every production of genius must be the production of enthusiasm.

—Benjamin Disraeli

Behold the turtle—he makes progress only when he sticks his neck out.

—Unknown

If you have built castles in the air, your work need not be lost; that is where they should be built. Now put foundations under them.

—Henry David Thoreau

Human beings can alter their lives by altering their attitudes of thought.

—William James

Have patience. All things are difficult before they become easy.

—Moslih Eddin Saadi

Three men were laying brick.
The first was asked: "What are you doing?"
He answered: "Laying some brick."
The second man was asked: "What are you working for?"
He answered: "Five dollars a day."
The third man was asked: "What are you doing?"
He answered: "I am helping to build a great cathedral."

—Charles M. Schwab

Be alive! Be enthusiastic! The word "enthusiasm" comes from a Greek word which means *to be inspired or possessed by the god* —a wonderful word for a wonderful quality.

Get excited about something! Perhaps, at the start, you may have to feign enthusiasm. If so, go right ahead! Tell yourself, "This is wonderful! I'm bound to succeed!" Soon you'll find that what started out as artificial, manufactured enthusiasm is now the real thing! Start *acting* enthusiastic and soon you'll *be* enthusiastic!

When April rains come, one man sees mud puddles. Another sees—flowers!

Perhaps our great stumbling block is the lack of belief in our own abilities. What we believe we cannot do, we can *not* do. What we believe we can do, we *can* do.

❧❧

Our *aliveness* can be measured by how much we want to know and how many things we desire to do.

❧❧

If you want life to give you more, make plans to give more of yourself to life.

❧❧

The happy, confident, cooperative attitude of a successful man is not the result of his success. His success is the result of his attitude.

❧❧

A deed performed is worth a score of resolutions.

❧❧

We gain the confidence of others through displaying confidence in ourselves.

❧❧

Let's beware if we find ourselves using progress-stoppers such as "difficult," "hard," "impossible," "I can't," "I won't," "I'm afraid," "I doubt," "I'm against," or "I don't believe." Use instead progress-makers such as "easy," "I can," "I know," "I will," and "I'm sure." These are words that built the world.

❧❧

The most important thing in the world to me *now* is what I am doing *now*, the most important thought that which I am thinking *now*, the most important person the person to whom I am talking *now*.

❧❧

You can visualize only one mental picture at a time. If you see yourself as being confident, you cannot simultaneously see yourself as lacking in confidence. If you picture yourself as being safe, you cannot at the same time see yourself as being in danger. Visualize positive, happy, confident mental pictures. You *are* the person you picture yourself as being!

❧❧

Let's act *as if* we were considerate of others, *as if* we were enthusiastic, *as if* we were interested in our job, *as if* we liked our neighbors, *as if* we were generous, *as if* we were brave, *as if* we were confident, *as if* we were happy. If we do this we *will be* considerate of others, we *will be* enthusiastic, we *will be* interested in our job, we *will like* our neighbors, we *will be* generous, we *will be* brave, we *will be* confident, and we *will be* happy. We are players who become like the parts which we act.

❧❧

Self-confidence comes first; then initiative.

❧❧

Those with failure patterns speak often of what is wrong with things and people. Those with success patterns talk primarily about what is right.

❧❧

One good action outweighs a thousand idle promises.

❧❧

When life hands you a difficulty that you view as a disadvantage, look for the opportunity that can lead to an advantage.

❧

When we get a negative thought, let's refuse to put it into words. Better yet, put the opposite, positive version into words and say those words aloud to ourselves or to others.

❧

Let's give ourselves powerful suggestions, such as these:

1. I *am* happy!
2. I *like* people!
3. I *am* enthusiastic!
4. I *am* a great salesman!

Or we can vary the form of these suggestions and use the method of expression that was used by Coué in the early part of the twentieth century: "Day by day in every way I'm getting

1. better and better!"
2. healthier and healthier!
3. happier and happier!
4. richer and richer!
5. to like people more and more!
6. to like speaking before groups more and more!

In phrasing these and similar affirmations, be sure that the suggestions are sufficiently realistic that they can be accepted as true. Also avoid stating them negatively. Don't say, "Day by day I'm forgetting less and less," but rather, "Day by day my memory is getting better and better." Negating the negative is not as powerful as asserting the positive! We should concentrate on the condition we desire, not on the one we are trying to eliminate!

We might develop one- and two-sentence "commercials" to tell ourselves how good we are, as an aid for various specific situations. If we are scheduled to give a speech, let's tell ourselves, "I know more about this particular phase of this subject than anyone in the audience. I have a real message for my audience that will help them."

Still another "commercial" we might use is, "I look good; I feel fine." Or, "I've got what it takes to succeed and I'm succeeding. I'm going on to greater success." Or, "I feel relaxed. Each day it is becoming easier for me to meet difficult situations with calmness." And here's a message to tell ourselves each morning before starting the day's work: "I have tremendous energy today. I will rapidly and easily finish whatever I set out to do."

When we are working on a specific objective it is a good idea to copy the corresponding affirmation on a 3 x 5 index card and carry it in a pocket. Then read the card and repeat the affirmation several times each day—especially right before bedtime so that our subconscious mind can work on it while we sleep. Each time the affirmation is repeated it must be done, not mechanically, but rather with the full certainty that our objective is even now in the process of being achieved.

We can make ourselves more alive! Let's work at selling and re-selling ourselves on the idea that we are even now in the process of achieving whatever we are trying to achieve.

❧❧

To become enthusiastic, study the subject about which you would like to be enthusiastic. To learn a subject well, develop enthusiasm for it. Enthusiasm leads to study which leads to knowledge which leads to enthusiasm. Put this chain reaction to greater use!

❧❧

Think positively and express thoughts positively! If a friend is about to take a trip we wouldn't say, "I hope you don't get killed," but rather, "I hope you have a safe journey." Similarly, let's never say to a customer who has been mistreated, or thinks he's been mistreated, "I hope this won't end our relationship," but rather, "I assure you that your future orders will be handled to your entire satisfaction." Why not think, talk, and write about the things we want to happen and avoid thinking, talking, and writing about the things we hope will not happen. *Make full use of the positive attitude.*

Try asking, "How would a self-confident person act in this situation?" Then act that way!

In expressing ideas, it is probably wise to begin such a statement by saying, "In my opinion . . ."

In the realm of action, however, more positive statements should be made. Let's say, "I will . . ." rather than, "I will try . . ."

If we work at our job *as if* it is interesting, we will find that it *is* interesting!

We should be careful of the impact created on others, or on ourselves, unintentionally, by our words. The expression "*practice* on the piano" has made a million boys and girls hate the piano. The expression "*play* the piano" could have made them love it.

Distrusting others causes the rejection of our greatest opportunities.

There are always many reasons why a thing *can't* be done. Let's concentrate on the one reason why it *can* be done.

Don't expend those energies in avoiding defeat that would be better spent in gaining the victory.

❧❧

Next time we are in a church or classroom, or are at a meeting, let's sit in the front row. At meetings and conferences let's make comments or ask questions. These are ways of acting confident—and if we *act* confident, we will *be* confident!

❧❧

Avoid negative words. Instead of speaking of a "problem," why not talk about a "challenge"? Instead of a "big expense" we might speak of our "big investment." Positive words develop confidence—others' confidence in us—our confidence in ourselves.

❧❧

With enthusiasm, if we keep it long enough, we surmount all obstacles and achieve our goals.

❧❧

If we dress, walk, smile, and talk as if we already have love, health, happiness, and success, we will find love, health, happiness, and success. We get what we want by acting as if we already have it.

❧❧

Say to yourself: "I have confidence in myself. I know that the power within me will make it possible to do any reasonable thing that I wish to do."

❧❧

The uniform worn by a policeman or by a soldier contributes to his sense of bravery. A nurse's uniform increases her sense of helpfulness.

Uniforms symbolize many things but they are always symbols of the finest characteristics of the profession they represent. A policeman or soldier by wearing the uniform that represents bravery *becomes* brave. The nurse in wearing the uniform of helpfulness *becomes* helpful.

If you and I will dress neatly in the manner of successful persons and if we will radiate a spirit of confidence, then we will *become* confident and successful. We *become* what we pretend we already *are*.

❦❦

Our attitude toward others is a reflection of our attitude toward ourselves. When we expect others to be unreliable and dishonest, we are reflecting a very poor opinion of our own reliability and honesty.

If our faith and confidence in others is in need of renovation, let's begin by improving our opinion of ourselves. When we love ourselves, when we are confident, when we are honest, when we have faith in ourselves and in the goodness of our motives, then we will like others, we will find them reliable and honest, and we will find that their motives are governed by unselfishness.

❦❦

Wouldn't it be a good idea to speak with exclamation points? If we speak enthusiastically we'll *be* enthusiastic!

❦❦

Would I rather have my job than any other job in the world? If I would not, can I either change my job or change my attitude? Can I make myself feel that I would rather do the kind of work I do than do anything else?

When a man works, not for the money, but for the love of working, he finds success and happiness. Let's work because *we want to do it!*

Why lose confidence in our ideas simply because they are opposed by almost everyone we know? The great discoveries of science, the great paintings, the great books, the great symphonies were produced by nonconformists. Eventually the world accepted and then admired.

There are so many successes that we believe are impossible for us to attain—so many skills, whether it be ice skating, public speaking, or stock market speculation, that we believe are beyond us.

With desire, determination, and hard work we can perform miracles! Let's not believe so firmly in the closely prescribed boundaries we place on our talents. *Believe instead that there are no walls, there are no boundaries, to the capabilities and achievements of a man with determination!*

Welcome difficulties! It is through meeting and overcoming problems that we increase our own capabilities. We develop personal power in proportion to the effort we expend to master problems.

What security did the American pioneers have when they headed their Conestoga wagons toward the West? They left all semblance of security behind them. They sought *opportunity*—opportunity to struggle to change a wilderness into a garden. In spite of the probability of death from Indians or disease, they created their own security based on their own abilities, activities, and courage. Where are the men today who will reject the offer of security that they have not created? Where are the men who know that security is false unless it is self-created and self-sustained? Where are today's pioneers?

❧❧

Evidence of too much caution in any field of activity is a sign of insecurity in that area.

❧❧

A pessimist looks at an opportunity and sees a problem; an optimist looks at a problem and sees an opportunity.

❧❧

Present an appearance of modesty to the world, but within the confines of your mind discard modesty and replace it with pride and confidence in your abilities.

❧❧

Have we an enemy among our friends? Is there someone who usually sees the worst in every occurrence, one who discourages us from attempting great things? Who among our friends *encourages* us and who *discourages* us?

❧❧

Too much rest is more harmful than too much work.

❧❧

Don't wait until you're in the mood. Do it now!

❧❧

If you offer me my choice of two men for a job, one who has tremendous ability but little enthusiasm or perseverance and the other who has only modest ability but who possesses a bubbling enthusiasm and a tenacious endurance that refuses to leave a job undone or half-done, I'll take that second man. The man of enthusiasm and endurance will complete each project. A job short of perfect but one that is done is preferable to the perfect job that never becomes a reality.

❦❦

Here's a formula for confidence-building. Make a list of things at which you excel—singing, preparing Chicken Marengo, gardening, wiggling the ears, and so forth. Carry this list in your pocket. If you have prepared the list thoughtfully, it will enumerate many things you do well and, as you feel it in your pocket or think of it, your confidence will increase.

❦❦

Keeping a scrapbook of complimentary notes and letters, and reading it periodically when one's spirits are depressed, is a workable method of retaining and elevating self-confidence.

❦❦

Blessed is the man who thinks of his work as play. Blessed is he who is engaged in work that offers him challenges and presents him with problems. For it is the meeting of challenges and the solving of problems that produces happiness. The harder one works, the greater is the yield of satisfaction and joy. And that which yields great amounts of satisfaction and joy is thought of as play.

❦❦

Happiness and productivity follow when we think primarily of what we can do rather than dwelling upon what we cannot, or think we cannot, do.

❦❦

Tomorrow will bring burdens or opportunities. Which arrives will be decided entirely by our viewpoint.

❧❧

Actions, not words, are the builders of a reputation.

❧❧

The man who works only for money is both cheating and being cheated. Somewhere there is a job that he could perform with delight, achieving as a by-product a deep satisfaction in his contribution to the work of the world.

❧❧

The man who keeps his mind on the thing to be done has no time to feel unsure, to develop a lack of confidence or to question his ability to do it.

❧❧

If our eyes stay busy looking for the best, we will give our imagination very little time to imagine the worst.

❧❧

Criticism often tells more about the critic than it does about the person, action, or thing he is criticizing.

❧❧

We become what we picture ourselves as already being if the picture we visualize is clear and we are confident of its reality.

❧❧

Beware of a great human weakness—that of keeping a receptive mind to those negative thinkers who offer us their brand of mental disease. Let's seek the company of those who look on the bright side of things—those who know good things are possible—those who work to make good things come true instead of reciting reasons why these things cannot be achieved.

❧❧

The man who says it can't be done is frequently interrupted by a self-starter who announces that he has just done it.

❧❧

It's fine to see things as they are; it's better yet to see things as they could be.

❧❧

Enthusiasm is faith caught on fire!

4

The Road to Success

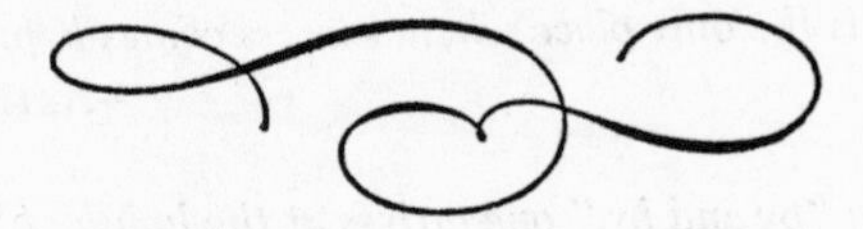

To laugh often and love much; to win the respect of intelligent people and the affection of children; to earn the approbation of honest critics and endure the betrayal of false friends; to appreciate beauty; to find the best in others; to give one's self; to leave the world a bit better, whether by a healthy child, a garden patch, or a redeemed social condition; to have played and laughed with enthusiasm and sung with exultation; to know even one life has breathed easier because you have lived—this is to have succeeded.

—Ralph Waldo Emerson

Successful people are dreamers who have found a dream too exciting, too important, to remain in the realm of fantasy. And who, day by day, hour by hour, toil in the service of their dream until they can touch it with their hands and see it with their eyes.

—Earl Nightingale

Dream lofty dreams, and as you dream, so shall you become. Your Vision is the promise of what you shall one day be; your Ideal is the prophecy of what you shall at last unveil.

The greatest achievement was at first and for a time a dream. The oak sleeps in the acorn; the bird waits in the egg; and in the highest vision of the soul a waking angel stirs. Dreams are the seedlings of realities.

—James Lane Allen

The gent who wakes up and finds himself a success hasn't been asleep.

—Wilson Mizner

Nothing succeeds so well as success.

—Alexander A. Talleyrand

The dictionary is the only place where success comes before work.

—Arthur Brisbane

By the streets of "by and by," one arrives at the house of "never."

—Saavedra M. de Cervantes

The world bestows its big prizes both in money and honors for but one thing. And that is initiative. And what is initiative? I'll tell you: it is doing the right thing without being told.

—Elbert Hubbard

Do not think that what is hard for thee to master is impossible for man; but if a thing is possible and proper to man, deem it attainable by thee.

—Marcus Aurelius Antoninus

If the day and the night are such that you greet them with joy, and life emits a fragrance like flowers and sweet-scented herbs, is more elastic, more starry, more immortal,—that is your success.

—Henry David Thoreau

Ah, but a man's reach should exceed his grasp,
Or what's a heaven for?

—Robert Browning

The man who insists upon seeing with perfect clearness before he decides, never decides.

—Henri-Frédéric Amiel

We all have to learn, in one way or another, that neither men nor boys get second chances in this world. We all get new chances to the end of our lives, but not second chances in the same set of circumstances; and the great difference between one person and another is how he takes hold and uses his first chance, and how he takes his fall if it is scored against him.

—THOMAS HUGHES

There is a kind of reverse perspective in opportunities; they always look larger when they are receding from us than when they are approaching us.

—SYDNEY J. HARRIS

The heights by great men won and kept
Were not attained by sudden flight
For they, while their companions slept,
Were toiling upwards in the night.

—HENRY WADSWORTH LONGFELLOW

It is not the critic who counts, not the man who points out how the strong man stumbled or where the doer of deeds could have done them better. The credit belongs to the man who is actually in the arena; whose face is marred by dust and sweat and blood; who strives valiantly; who errs and comes up short again and again; who knows the great enthusiasms, the great devotions, and spends himself in a worthy cause; who at the best knows in the end the triumph of high achievement; and who at the worst, if he fails, at least fails while daring greatly; so that his face shall never be with those cold and timid souls who know neither defeat nor victory.

—THEODORE ROOSEVELT

A lazy man is never lucky.

—PERSIAN PROVERB

In great attempts it is glorious even to fail.

—LONGINUS

The truest wisdom, in general, is a resolute determination.

—NAPOLEON BONAPARTE

In every field of human endeavor, he that is first must perpetually live in the white light of publicity. Whether the leadership be vested in a man or in a manufactured product, emulation and envy are ever at work. In art, in literature, in music, in industry, the reward and the punishment are always the same. The reward is widespread recognition; the punishment, fierce denial and detraction. When a man's work becomes a standard for the whole world, it also becomes a target for the shafts of the envious few. If his work be merely mediocre, he will be left severely alone—if he achieve a masterpiece, it will set a million tongues a-wagging. Jealousy does not protrude its forked tongue at the artist who produces a commonplace painting. Whatsoever you write, or paint, or play, or sing, or build, no one will strive to surpass or to slander you, unless your work be stamped with the seal of genius. Long, long after a great work or a good work has been done, those who are disappointed or envious continue to cry out that it cannot be done. Spiteful little voices in the domain of art were raised against our own Whistler as a mountebank, long after the big world had acclaimed him its greatest artistic genius. Multitudes flocked to Bayreuth to worship at the musical shrine of Wagner, while the little group of those whom he had dethroned and displaced argued angrily that he was no musician at all. The little world continued to protest that Fulton could never build a steamboat, while the big world flocked to the river banks to see his boat steam by. The leader is assailed because he is a leader, and the effort to equal him is merely added proof of that leadership. Failing to equal or to excel, the follower seeks to depreciate and to destroy—but only confirms once more the superiority of that which he strives to supplant.

There is nothing new in this. It is as old as the world and as old as the human passions—envy, fear, greed, ambition, and the desire to surpass. And it all avails nothing. If the leader truly leads, he remains—the leader. Master-poet, master-painter, master-workman, each in his turn is assailed, and each holds his laurels through the ages. That which is good or great makes itself known, no matter how loud the clamor of denial. That which deserves to live—lives.

—This text appeared as an advertisement in *The Saturday Evening Post*, January 2nd, in the year 1915. Copyright, Cadillac Motor Car Company.

In truth, people can generally make time for what they choose to do: it is not really the time but the will that is lacking.

—Sir John Lubbock

On the whole, it is patience which makes the final difference between those who succeed or fail in all things. All the greatest people have it in an infinite degree, and among the less, the patient weak ones always conquer the impatient strong.

—John Ruskin

If you want a place in the sun you must expect some blister.

—Ted Malone

There are two forms of success. The one is achieved by having our fellow men work to further our ends. The other involves the devotion of self to furthering the ends of our fellow men.

What do we want out of life? What do we value most? What gives us our great satisfactions? Are we spending our time and effort to achieve the things we ourselves value, or are we giving our greatest effort to achieve ends valued not by ourselves but by our family, our neighbors, our boss, or our friends? In order to spend our time and effort most efficiently, let's first discover what the things are that we value and what the things are that we wish to achieve.

Luck is the preparation for, recognition of, and prompt seizure of opportunity.

❧

The ball player who would get to second base must take the risk of leaving first base.

❧

Try to see opportunity where others see only occurrences, phenomena, and facts. But don't merely *see* opportunities, *act* on them!

❧

Let's not keep telling ourselves or let others tell us reasons why we can't do something that we want to do. All we need is one good reason why it is possible—then just go right ahead and do it!

❧

The unsuccessful person is one who habitually plans to do it later and, planning to do it *later*, he does it *never*. The successful man believes in *doing it now*. In fact, see, it is already done!

❧

Why must caution and procrastination cause you to lose? Next time don't say that "common sense" demands that you decline the opportunity. Next time call it *fear*. And having unmasked fear and called it by name, let "common sense," not fear, decide.

❧

A man is successful if he is doing his best. A second man may surpass him but if that second man is falling short of his own best possible performance, then he is the less successful. Success refers not so much to the winning but to how the race is run.

❧❧

"Luck" is the outsider's evaluation of another's determination, hard work, courage, and skill.

❧❧

To maximize the achievement, minimize the time between the decision and the act.

❧❧

All progress is the result of some man's discontent put into action. Things as they are are never the best.

❧❧

If you can't be best, be second best. If you can't do a lot, do a little. Do what you can.

❧❧

There are many trails that lead to the top of the mountain. But the view from the summit is experienced only by those who took the first step and then another and then another.

❧❧

How do we achieve successes? *By analyzing our failures.* It is through learning to profit from our mistakes that we improve our success-failure ratio.

❧❧

Success comes to those who do things rather than to those who merely talk about doing things, to those who do rather than to those who just wish, to those who do it *now* rather than to those who delay. Success follows action, not inaction.

❦

Great success is composed of a series of little successes. The little job is a link that builds the chain. Do it well!

❦

We cannot fail until we have made our last try. Let's not make our last try until we have succeeded.

❦

I'm going to think about the reasons why I can succeed in each venture I consider—and ignore that long list of reasons why I can't. Attitude, not intelligence, is the great success-maker.

❦

Listen to advice—but make your own decisions.

❦

We achieve our major goals by successfully achieving the smaller subgoals. If the housewife's goal is a clean house, she achieves it by cleaning one room at a time. The writer completes his book by achieving successive subgoals in the form of pages or of chapters. The salesman exceeds his monthly quota by successfully achieving subgoals of above-quota weeks.

To help us keep on achieving our subgoals, we should promise ourselves rewards. If the housewife promises to reward herself with a cup of coffee after cleaning the bedrooms, she has provided an incentive to complete the task as rapidly as possible. The writer who refuses to smoke until he has finished a page but, as he writes, keeps promising himself a reward in the form of a cigarette as soon as the page is completed will finish that page in short order. The salesman who promises himself that he will play golf on Saturday if he has an above-quota week has an incentive to keep working hard and long each day to help earn his week-end reward.

To win the major goals, we must achieve each subgoal. To achieve the subgoals, let's promise ourselves rewards.

❧❧

With each job we tackle let's ask ourselves, "How can I do more than I am expected to do?" Wouldn't it be a good idea to give the boss, our friends, and strangers more effort, more friendliness, more of all good things than they expect to receive?

❧❧

You say it can't be done? Turn around and somebody's done it!

❧❧

Let's put our goals in concrete form. If we are trying to lose weight, we might try to find an old photo taken in our slender days and paste it up on the refrigerator door. How can we eat those fat-making snacks while staring at that picture!

If we are saving for a home, why not carry in our wallet an illustration of a home similar to the one about which we're dreaming? It will act as an effective padlock on our wallet when we are tempted to make some frivolous expenditures.

Let's put our goals on paper and make sure that piece of paper is constantly before us to act as an inspiration.

❧❧

I am confident. I can achieve whatever I attempt to do.

The most difficult thing to do is to make a start. Progress toward great achievements begins, as does any journey, with a single step.

❧❧

Success materializes through my expectation that it will occur. And so does failure.

❧

Security is the will-of-the-wisp chased by wishers. Perhaps there may be security in death; but there is no security in life. And if there were, it would not be desirable! Happiness is achieved only through continual, never-ending struggles to attain worth-while goals.

❧

There is a time for dreams and a time for thought and a time for action.

❧

Why not take "I can" for our motto? Let's act as if failure is impossible. If we sincerely believe that success is inevitable, we will experience a tremendous increase in drive and perseverance, and success will be ours!

❧

Make decisions! Solve problems as they come up! When vital facts are likely to become known later, there may be good reasons to delay a decision. But when it is unlikely that new facts will become available, let's act now! We must learn to accept our mistakes and to tell ourselves that a wrong action or a wrong solution to a problem is better than no action at all. When we make a mistake, we learn something. When we put off taking action and put off making a decision, we are trying to escape from life by letting fate and time decide for us. Meet life's problems with action!

❧

Luck rewards those who work as if it did not exist.

❧❧

The longest journey is made *one mile at a time.* The greatest success starts with a single trial and is finally achieved only after a cyclic succession of trials, mistakes, and minor achievements. Go the first mile—make that first trial now!

❧❧

Learn to be unafraid of failure. Welcome failure as a sign that you have tried something beyond your normal capabilities and congratulate yourself for having made the effort. Failures harden us and teach us things that are impossible to learn through successes.

❧❧

Consider what these have in common:

1. Making a living by playing the horses
2. Running a 4-minute mile
3. Consistently making profits on both the long and short side of the stock market
4. Building a million dollar business on a thousand dollar investment
5. Knowing the name of everyone in your town.

Here's what these endeavors have in common: they are conceded to be extremely difficult—impossible for more than a few men to achieve.

An exciting way to live is to select a project that is considered to be impossible—one that virtually everybody agrees cannot be done. Then apply study, determination, and hard work—and just go right ahead and do it!

❧❧

Let's not laugh off hunches. Hunches are often the end product of considerable experience and of thought on a subconscious level.

Do not ignore them without first evaluating the risks and opportunities involved. If the risk is slight and the opportunity is great, let's act on that hunch!

❦

Are we looking for a formula for avoiding criticism? That's simple! Just *do nothing!* Only the doers are criticized. The active persons —those who are accomplishing things—are the ones who meet with disapproval.

When the doer is not criticized he will be dead. But the man who is doing things is too busy to concern himself with the caustic remarks of those who are not.

❦

We are "successful" when we arrive at goals we have set for ourselves. Virtually every success we achieve is accomplished through the cooperation of others. Since cooperation of others is a most important element in achieving success, isn't it especially vital to earn their friendship?

In all our driving to attain success, let's not forget to be kind and generous to those around us. From a purely selfish standpoint, the rewards of unselfishness are great.

❦

We will accomplish more and live happier lives if we periodically set aims for ourselves and write them down. By setting such aims we will tremendously increase our determination and our abilities.

Suppose we ask ourselves what we would like to have and what we would like to be a few years from now. Then ask if it is reasonable to hope to attain these aims. We should not be dismayed if our objectives are somewhat above our immediate capabilities since directed effort can increase our abilities. However, let's not set our sights so high that success is virtually impossible.

Instead, set possible aims for ourselves and then, after they are achieved, we can establish new and higher goals.

After our aims are determined, we subdivide these principal aims into secondary objectives. Then, next to each of these subgoals, let's set down the specific procedures, education, or experience needed to realize it. Estimate the amount of time needed to achieve each subgoal and record it. Finally, we keep reviewing this timetable for success and do our best to keep on schedule.

When our mind is not otherwise occupied, let's think of our immediate objective and remind ourselves of the advantages of achieving it. We can take pride as we successfully complete steps toward attaining each objective. We should continue to tell ourselves that success will soon be ours. Happiness is the by-product of the effort to attain our goals.

❦❦

The measure of our performance should be, not the other man's performance, but our own best effort and our own potential. Analyze what *we* have done, and are doing in terms of what *we* can do. Let's compete with ourselves and with our finest capabilities. Success is the reward we achieve for making our accomplishments match our possibilities.

❦❦

"Good luck" is the term the world gives to the amalgamation of knowledge, skill, bravado, and hard work after time has completed the chemistry and produced *success*.

❦❦

How can you make progress in your job? By looking for the difficult projects, the ones no one else wants to tackle, the ones others can't do! Search for these projects, and when you find one of them say, "Let me do it!"

❧

Is there a universal method for achieving financial success? If there is, perhaps it is the technique of following proven business methods enough of the time so that sufficient profits are made to permit some gambling. The secret seems to lie in directing some funds away from the safe and steady business operation to occasional speculation on the wildcat, the longshot, the high-risk, high-gain proposition, the impossible experiment that, if successful—as some day one will be—wealth follows.

❧

The man who accepts only the jobs that he can do well enough to avoid criticism will accept no jobs.

❧

Let's think less about what we want and more about our plan to get what we want.

❧

A successful person is successful because he operates his own efficient "luck factory." He manufactures luck by preparing for opportunities, by recognizing opportunities when they arrive, and by promptly acting on them.

❧

If you wait for the boss to *give* you responsibility, you are apt to see that responsibility *taken* by a more aggressive associate who is in the process of moving to the top.

❧

Security is less related to the possession of material wealth than to the ability to create wealth.

❧❧

Great success is achieved through great risk. Only through exposing ourselves to new, unfamiliar experiences where greater failure is possible can we hope to achieve greater success.

If we are willing to fail, study that failure and try again, then fail again, study that failure and try again, we will succeed! Each time we fail we learn how *not* to do it. It is these lessons that make our failures so valuable. Failure is the best friend of success. One must not fear failure, but welcome it as an essential ingredient in the making of success. However, let's never allow a failure to go unstudied; only the studied failures pull us along the road to our success.

❧❧

Action and accomplishment frequently consume less time and energy than our explanations excusing our lack of action and accomplishment. Actions build, excuses detract from, our own opinions of ourselves. And it is our own opinions of ourselves that are so vital in determining what others think of us.

❧❧

A project worked at half-heartedly in expectation of failure is almost certain to end in failure. Something becomes possible for us to achieve only *after* we sincerely believe it is possible for us to achieve it.

❧❧

It is easier to *get* what we want out of life than to *decide* what we want out of life. The man who has a singularity of purpose—whether it be the desire to be rich, to be educated, or to be well-liked by others—will, if he devotes all his energies to that purpose, achieve his objective. What we *get* out of life is determined by what we decide we *want* out of life.

❧❧

What are the great factors that determine the success or failure of any venture? Our attitude toward that venture, our belief in ourselves and in those others who must help us, our enthusiasm to do actively what must be done, and the degree of our certainty that success is inevitable.

❧❧

Failure to act is more often a result of fear than of wisdom.

❧❧

You can't get to first base if you're playing basketball.

❧❧

How can we insure that we will receive salary increases and job promotions? By making certain we always give more and better service than is expected; by working so productively that we are always *underpaid*. The extra time we invest in doing what is *not* expected and for which we are not paid will yield the biggest eventual return on our investment.

❧❧

The most valuable employees of any business are those who start things before they are asked to do so. The least valuable are those who won't do what they're told and those who *won't do anything else!*

❧❧

Those who work to diminish their discontent achieve success and happiness. Others who merely worry about their discontent find failure and unhappiness. Discontent is normal and necessary to the progress of the world. It is our decision to worry or to work toward the elimination of this discontent that determines our destiny.

Successful men reach decisions rapidly and are inclined to change a decision only after a considerable weight of evidence indicates a change is in order. Unsuccessful men reach decisions slowly and are inclined to change their decisions quickly with very little reason. We should try to reach decisions rapidly—just as soon as the pertinent data or evidence is available. And once we have reached a decision, let's devote our energies to carrying it out, rather than to worrying as to whether or not the decision was correct.

Men who are unwilling to take a chance are left those of life's opportunities that remain after others have made their choice.

If he was lucky twice, it wasn't luck but ability.

Those who love the work more than the money will make more of the money.

Do not wait for opportunity to knock. Successful men go out and look for opportunities, and when they can't *find* opportunities they wish to accept, they *make* their own.

Those who keep doing the impossible long enough find that it's possible.

Success is achieved by first deciding to stop doing the things that we know we shouldn't be doing in order to make time to do the things that we know we should be doing.

Every successful man is indebted to one or more persons who inspired him to great achievement. He remains in debt to mankind until he, in turn, helps someone else attain success.

5

The Development of Character

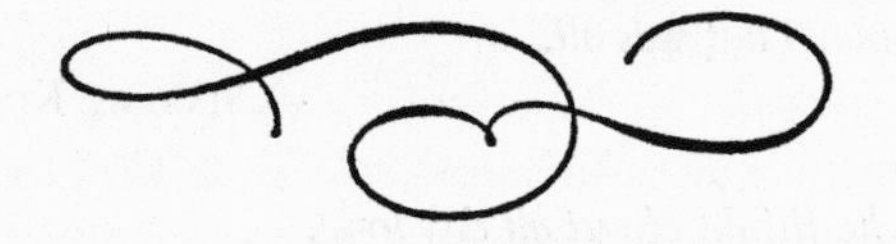

A man's face, as Lincoln puts it, is his own fault after forty. What makes your face the way it is, is what you spend your evenings thinking.

—Archibald MacLeish

Judge not, that ye be not judged.

—Jesus (Matthew 7:1)

If you tell me how you get your feeling of importance, I'll tell you what you are. That determines your character.

—Dale Carnegie

Grant that I may not so much
Seek to be consoled as to console;
To be understood as to understand;
To be loved as to love.
For it is in giving that we receive!

—St. Francis of Assisi

The tragedy of life is in what dies inside a man while he lives—the death of genuine feeling, the death of inspired response, the death of the awareness that makes it possible to feel the pain or the glory of other men in yourself.

—NORMAN COUSINS

Why are the saints, saints? Because they were cheerful, when it was difficult to be cheerful, patient, when it was diffiicult to be patient; and because they pushed on when they wanted to stand still, and kept silent when they wanted to talk, and were agreeable when they wanted to be disagreeable. That was all.

—CHARLES KELLOGG FIELD

A man is what he thinks about all day long.

—RALPH WALDO EMERSON

Dishonesty is a forsaking of permanent for temporary advantages.

—CHRISTIAN NESTELL BOVEE

It is a thing very possible that a man should be a very divine man, and yet be altogether unknown.

—MARCUS AURELIUS ANTONINUS

This above all: to thine own self be true, and it must follow, as the night the day, thou canst not then be false to any man.

—WILLIAM SHAKESPEARE

Kites rise against and not with the wind.

—JOHN NEAL

If there is to be any regeneration of our people, it must take place in the small laboratories of our private lives. We must realize with all the intensity we can command, that re-fashioning our own character is not only the most satisfying and rewarding preoccupation of man, but is also the most important contribution we can make to society.

—DR. ALEXIS CARREL

Sow an act, and you reap a habit; sow a habit, and you reap a character; sow a character, and you reap a destiny.

—Bishop Jeremy Taylor

He who sacrifices his conscience to ambition burns a picture to obtain the ashes.

—Chinese proverb

Have you learned lessons only of those who admired you, and were tender with you, and stood aside for you? Have you not learned great lessons from those who rejected you, and braced themselves against you, or disputed the passage with you?

—Walt Whitman

Anyone can become angry—that is easy; but to be angry with the right person, and to the right degree, and at the right time, and for the right purpose, and in the right way—that is not within everybody's power and is not easy.

—Aristotle

Honesty isn't any policy at all; it's a state of mind or it isn't honesty.

—Eugene L'Hôte

Wealth is not only what you have *but it is also what you* are.

—Sterling W. Sill

The superior man ranks the effort above the prize, and worthiness to be known above being known.

—Confucius

What a man thinks of himself, that it is which determines, or rather indicates, his fate.

—Henry David Thoreau

The superior man makes demands upon himself; the inferior man makes demands upon others.

—Confucius

He flattered himself on being a man without any prejudices; and this pretension itself is a very great prejudice.

—ANATOLE FRANCE

Character is like a tree and reputation like its shadow. The shadow is what we think of it; the tree is the real thing.

—ABRAHAM LINCOLN

One man with courage makes a majority.

—ANDREW JACKSON

Don't permit yourself to show temper, and always remember that when you are in the right you can afford to keep your temper and when you are in the wrong you cannot afford to lose it.

J. J. REYNOLDS

There is a saying in the theatre that everyone's second business is show business, but it must be unmistakable by now that I think everyone's second business is their occupation and that their first business is to know themselves.

—JO COUDERT

Every man has within himself a continent of undiscovered character. Happy is he who proves the Columbus of his soul.

—JOHANN WOLFGANG VON GOETHE

If of thy mortal goods thou art bereft,
And from thy slender store two loaves alone to thee are left,
Sell one, and with the dole
Buy hyacinths to feed thy soul.

—MOSLIH EDDIN SAADI

The great scientific discoveries of the past hundred years have been as child's play compared with the titanic forces that will be released when man applies himself to the understanding and mastery of his own nature.

—MELVIN J. EVANS

The only birds that talk are parrots, and they don't fly very high.

—WILBUR WRIGHT

Granted that it is difficult, appallingly so at times, to be sure exactly who you are, and granted also that there is a sense in which every man ought to live as if he were on the way to becoming a different person than what he now is—the truth remains that all mental and spiritual health begins with self-acceptance.

—STEPHEN F. BAYNE, JR.

If you would improve mankind's character begin by improving your own.

❦❦

We cannot hope to control all the things that may happen to us, but we can seek to control our reactions to them.

❦❦

When there are alternative courses of action let's take the one that makes us proud of ourselves—or at least not ashamed.

❦❦

Does not the ethical man praise an object that he plans to buy just as freely as he praises one that he desires to sell?

❦❦

Never let a man change your opinion of men.

❦

The spread of gossip requires not only a talker but a listener. Is the attentive ear less guilty than the wagging tongue?

❦

The heat of anger is quenched by the coolness of silence.

❦

To help ourselves to stay on a diet, or to practice thrift, or to summon strength for saying "no" to a cocktail, or to cure ourselves of any bad habit, all we need do is ask ourselves, "Can't I refrain from eating this food (or buying this item, or taking this drink) for just another twenty-four hours?" Let's not force ourselves to give up bad habits; just postpone practice of the habit for another twenty-four hours, then another twenty-four, then another.

❦

Can we learn to hate anger but not the angry person, greed but not the greedy, gluttony but not the glutton? Can we learn to hate the crime but not the criminal?

❦

What are we seeking in others? Are we looking for beauty? We will find it! Are we looking for ugliness? We will find it! Are we looking for honesty? We will find it! Are we looking for dishonesty? We will find it!

When we meet others do we look for smiles? We will find smiles! Do we look for friendliness? We will find friendliness! For what are we searching? We will find it! Life brings to us what we bring to life.

❧

In being late for an appointment we waste another's most precious possession—his time.

❧

In an argument there may be two correct answers or two incorrect answers to match the two different viewpoints of the arguers. The "winner" of an argument, the one who avoids conflict and tension, the one who leaves his mind open to another point of view, is the one who says, "I may be wrong."

❧

It is the hard job, so distasteful in contemplation, that is so pleasant in retrospect. Let's welcome difficult projects.

❧

Why should I be reluctant to say I was wrong? Should I be ashamed of my capacity to learn?

❧

When we spill milk on the floor and must clean it up—when we must wait for that mile-long freight train—when we are interrupted while reading—why not welcome the experience? Continual tests of our patience make it strong. Let's welcome those inconveniences that build our P.Q.—our Patience Quotient.

❧

The word "tolerance" seems to be used sometimes, quite improperly, to denote a lack of conviction as to what is right and wrong. Perhaps in our thinking about crimes of men and of nations we need more of the "intolerance" displayed by Jesus in driving the money-changers from the temple. Tolerance is not a synonym for indifference and should not be so equated in our minds.

✻✻

The greatness of a man is indicated by the number of good words he has for his colleagues and competitors.

✻✻

Remember each favor received; forget each one you do.

✻✻

Are the words I am about to speak superior to the silence? I am the master of my unspoken words. I am the slave of those words that should have remained unsaid.

✻✻

Next time I am in disagreement with someone I'll say, "I've made a lot of mistakes and will make a lot more. This may be just another one of the many times I've been wrong." Chances are he'll reply, "I may be the one who's mistaken." Thus the way is cleared for friendly, less emotional, more thoughtful discussion.

✻✻

The most serious way in which a person can hurt me is to make me hate him. I will forget. If I cannot forget, I will forgive.

✻✻

Stop asking *who* is right and try, instead, to determine *what* is right.

✻✻

Life gives to us what we give to life. Life is a mirror reflecting ourselves.

❧❧

The cheerful news, the friendly thoughts, the creative ideas that I get today I will share with others. My problems, my aches and pains, I will not readily share with anyone.

❧❧

Why should you and I fear the man who is loud, blustering, and domineering? Why should we fear the desk-pounder, the man who violently asserts that an opinion, a method, an idea other than his own is impossible? Pity him; he is suffering from a too-keen sense of his own inferiority.

❧❧

Let's try to convert *feeling* into *thinking* whenever we feel angry, embarrassed, or self-conscious. Let's try to analyze the *feeling* that we are experiencing. The analysis necessary to label it "anger," "embarrassment," or "self-consciousness" will cause the undesirable feeling to disappear.

❧❧

Anger was a valuable survival trait for early man. Those of our ancestors who, when cornered by wild animals, did not become angry and did not put up a good fight failed to survive. Today this useful function for anger no longer exists but, like a man's appendix, anger continues as part of our makeup. Nowadays the best decisions are based not on angry deeds but on intelligent action. Let's calm down before we speak. In an angry situation silence often makes the most valuable contribution.

❧❧

The word "mad" is a better synonym for "angry" than language students believe it to be. Anger is the sane man's imitation of insanity.

Almost all of us have to be on constant guard to avoid exaggeration. Exaggeration is, in fact, so common that we all tend to believe that virtually everything we hear is somewhat overstated.

Don't you think our friends and associates would be pleasantly relieved to find someone who would simply state facts without exaggeration, one who erred on the side of understatement?

Where a display of knowledge may on occasion cause envy, a frank admission of the lack of knowledge often evokes admiration.

Modesty is the father of envy. The modest person, who visualizes himself as being inferior, envies others whom be believes to be superior. The cure for modesty is self-confidence which, once attained, requires for its sustenance neither an air of modesty nor of superiority.

An appearance of modesty may at times be a socially commendable trait. But, inwardly, let's attain a degree of self-confidence that, although permitting *external* modesty, cannot coexist with *internal* modesty.

Let's help solve the problems of our church, our school, our community *after* we have met the needs of our own families for love, encouragement, and appreciation. We ought to work for our church, our school, and our community, but only *after* we have attempted to create the same fineness of character in ourselves that we would create for our church, our school, and for our community. Helping to change the world is commendable *after* we have completed the necessary changes in ourselves.

❦

The young person of nine or ninety finds the past less attractive than either the present or the future. The old person of nine or ninety feels that all good things ended the day before yesterday.

❦

Another's anger remains non-contagious if we pretend that we do not notice it.

❦

If I would destroy a man, I must cause him to hate me. But I must continue to love him or I will destroy myself. Could a man understand this paradox and still hate?

❦

Who lost the argument? Two men—two hearts—two stomachs.

❦

An argument differs from a discussion in several important ways. An argument is emotional; a discussion is intellectual. In an argument neither arguer is ever convinced by the other; in a discussion one may be convinced by the other or each may come to see that the other's points have validity. In an argument each tries to make the other feel inferior, to prove him wrong or even foolish; in a discussion there is no compulsion to demonstrate the inferiority of the other person.

Only victims of an inferiority complex can engage in an argument. Such persons feel insecure and cannot endure the thought of being wrong. They feel compelled to dismiss all possibility of their being in error and will violently defend whatever position they have taken. On the other hand, the superior person who is confident of his talent recognizes the relativity of opinions. He does not feel insulted if someone expresses ideas contrary to his own. He is not humiliated if the other man's view is shown to be correct and his own opinion is proved to be wrong. His objective is to learn—not to defend a wrong position.

The superior person acts on the words of Jesus, "Agree with thine adversary quickly" (Matthew 5:25), and in those cases when he must disagree he does so without being disagreeable. An argument can never be won but it can be avoided.

❧❧

The ancient Greeks erected a statue and inscribed it "To the Unknown God." With all of their numerous gods who controlled every conceivable phenomenon, human and natural, they were ready to admit they might not have the total answer to spiritual problems. Why not assume, as did the ancient Greeks, that in our spiritual and ethical outlook we may not necessarily be 100 per cent correct and that the Moslems, the Hindus, the Buddhists, the Indians of the Guatemalan Highlands may not be 100 per cent wrong? To be tolerant is commendable, but let's go beyond tolerance and try to *appreciate* the beliefs and opinions of others.

❧❧

The man who builds his life around a desire for revenge will find that life has its revenge on him as he reaps the sorrow and unhappiness he has sowed.

❧❧

Next time someone becomes angry with you, quietly and calmly accept the opportunity being offered you to make an on-the-spot study of an angry person, his actions and his reactions to your calmness. Concentrate your attention, not on what *you* may be feeling, but on what *he* is saying and doing.

❧

The quality of a man is measured not only by what he is and does but by what he aspires to be and to do.

❧

Men who know the most say "I don't know" the most.

❧

What we think about, what we visualize as our ideal, we will become.

❧

The quality of one's character determines, to a large degree, the events that will befall him. To evil men come the bad events, to men of goodwill come the good.

❧

Through revenge we can "get even" with an enemy; through forgiveness we can become superior to him.

❧

Let's never allow another's reaction to our words and actions cause us to become angry. Instead, we should seek to understand why this person is displaying an unpleasant reaction.

Very likely something we said or did was at least partially at fault. Seldom is it possible to appreciate fully the causes of another's behavior. We must assume, however, that we would sympathize with that behavior if we could get inside his skin and understand what is causing his reaction.

Quite possibly he is reacting not only to our words and actions but to his own feeling of inferiority—and remember that aggression is one of the more usual reactions people display in an attempt to hide their inferiority feelings. Aggression is often used in an attempt to hide fear. Dogmatic statements are frequently employed to hide uncertainty.

When we view another's unpleasantness as an object for analysis and we study diligently in an attempt to understand him, then we cannot become angry ourselves.

❦❦

It is stimulating to associate occasionally with those who act and speak in ways that we find irritating. This very irritation may indicate that we are about to discover a new viewpoint—a new approach to life and its problems. The measure of our maturity is not in our ability to avoid reacting but in our ability to control our reactions.

❦❦

To be *un*satisfied is to be alert to the possibility of improvement. To be *dis*satisfied is to dissipate our energies in maintaining a state of frustration.

❦❦

Forgiveness is a gift that benefits the giver even more than it benefits the receiver. Forgiveness refused hurts the refuser more than it does the refused.

❦❦

Apply the principle "appearances may be deceiving" whenever we are confronted with a seemingly bad action. Refrain from conclusion-jumping; assume the act may have been motivated by good intentions.

❦❦

When we are criticized and we know the criticism is warranted, we ought to admit it and ask for help in overcoming the objection.

If we are not sure whether the criticism is valid let's, after we are no longer with our critic, write down what he said and think about it until we can form a judgment as to its validity.

When we are criticized unjustly and we are positive that the criticism is not valid, why let it cause us to worry? A man who criticizes us unjustly has, by his words, told more about *himself* than he's told about *us*. Maybe he has told us enough so that we can be of help to him.

❦❦

Next time we find ourselves faced with annoying circumstances we might try to view the occurrence from the vantage point of the future. Tomorrow, next week, or next year, in recalling this situation aren't we apt to think of it, not as tragic, but as funny? If our answer is "Yes," then let's try to laugh off these annoyances *right now!*

❦❦

An injured person has a tremendous power over the person who has caused him the injury. He has the power to forgive.

❦❦

An ability that distinguishes successful from unsuccessful living is the ability to do what we should do when we should do it whether or not we desire to do it.

❦❦

Let us beware if our interest in books surpasses our interest in people. Remember the words of Alexander Pope, "The proper study of mankind is man."

❦❦

Reject the common fallacy that "blowing one's top" is the healthful way to temper anger. Children do it; mature adults do not.

❧

If someone does something or says harsh words that cause you to become angry, try meeting the situation with silence. Be thankful that in the matter of temper control and in thoughtfulness of others you are superior to the person angering you. Try to help him be calm by being calm and friendly yourself.

❧

Is honesty always the best policy? Perhaps not. Is it good human relations to tell your wife that she has an ugly hat when she seeks your admiration? When enemy soldiers enter the house and ask if any women are here do we tell them our seventeen-year-old niece is hiding upstairs? Or do we lie? Is it wise to be honest when truth will accomplish nothing but injury to another person? *Honesty is the best policy when others are helped, not injured, by our words.*

❧

Next time someone bungles a job for which we have given him instructions, let's not be too hasty to blame him. If anyone deserves the blame for a job poorly done it may be ourselves. If we had taught well, our student would have learned.

❧

More of our thoughts should remain unspoken. Next time we think negatively about some person or his action, let's be silent. We gain stature not only by what we say but by what we leave unsaid.

❧

Physical activity is a fine means for tempering anger, for making it possible for us to think more objectively about the person or problem that made us angry.

❧

We should not be concerned too much with what others will think of our actions. Rather, let's decide what we will think of ourselves if we take a given course of action or fail to take that action. To act in accord with the picture we paint of ourselves is a prerequisite to happy relations with others. Only if we are pleased with ourselves can we get along well with others.

❧

We hurt ourselves far more than we do our enemies when we try to "get even" with them. An enemy is a friend who does not understand us and whom we do not understand. Let's try to understand him and devote our energy toward getting him to understand us.

❧

Any man can display anger but the wise man won't. He knows that the injury to his heart and mind is too great a price to pay for any momentary satisfaction he may derive from such a display of anger. Calmness and forgiveness are signposts on Happiness Highway.

❧

Realize that ingratitude is natural and that only a minority show thankfulness on many occasions where an expression of gratitude would be in order. Expect ingratitude and do not worry about it. Give for the joy of giving, not for the pleasure of hearing, "Thank you."

❧

Do not be too hasty about labeling a belief "superstition." By using configurations of the planets similar to those discussed in astrology (a subject that is frequently labeled "superstition"), John H.

Nelson of R.C.A. Communications, Inc., predicts planetary influence on the sun's radiation which has a tremendous influence, in turn, upon radio reception and transmission. Nelson can predict months (or years) in advance the exact time when radio reception will be poor. Can we dogmatically insist that the planets do not exert an influence over other human affairs?

Are you certain that prediction of longevity by means of palm reading is nothing but superstition? Research conducted at Tulane University has demonstrated a similarity of palm-line patterns in those suffering from congenital heart defects.

Centuries ago high priests of several South American Indian tribes chewed coca leaves and spat the juice on a patient's body where an operation was to be performed. Would you condemn this "superstitious" practice? The leaf of the coca plant contains cocaine which anesthetized the area where the incision was to be made. *Let's be cautious about giving beliefs and strange practices the label "superstition."*

The weatherman predicts "partly cloudy"; preferably think "partly sunny." To some a glass may be "half empty"; instead think of it as "half full." Look on the bright side! Avoid negative thinking! Think positively!

The Apostle Paul tells us that the Athenians had a monument inscribed "To the Unknown God." Let's try to appreciate the open-mindedness back of that inscription dealing with an area where even today—after over 2,000 years—many minds are closed.

Let us form visions in our minds of other monuments. One of these could be inscribed, "To the painters of paintings I do not appreciate whom the world will some day call great." Another might read, "To the authors of novels and of poems which I find incomprehensible, but which will be read with appreciation by my children's children." A third monument could bear the words, "To men of good will everywhere whom I fail to understand. I will try to see through their eyes, hear through their ears, think as they think. Failing in my blindness and in my deafness and because of my mental limitations to assume their position, I will be tolerant—for it is my own shortcomings that cause my failure to appreciate their actions and their ideas."

❧❧

Anger is the name we give the bargaining process of trading three minutes of evil for three years of regret.

❧❧

Men of good will find good will in all men.

❧❧

Seize opportunity when it comes but be sure it is not an opportunity to take advantage of someone.

❧❧

Too much of our energy is spent in worry and concern that we may be deceived by others. As our ethical sense matures, our energies will be increasingly directed toward making sure we do not mislead others.

❧❧

Ask yourself, "Am I the kind of man my parents hoped I'd be?—the kind of husband my wife wants me to be?—the kind of father my children think I am?—the kind of person I'd like each of my children to grow up to be?"

❧❧

Before we take an action or react to someone else's action, let's ask ourselves how the person we would like to become would act or react.

❧❧

I will try to be honest, generous, and forgiving and to exemplify other good traits not only because I desire to help and to please others but because I desire to strengthen such traits in my own character.

My good acts may not be appreciated by others but such acts never go unrewarded. Each good act has its effect in developing, in strengthening, my character.

6

Helping Others

In the very act of giving, I experience my strength, my wealth, my power. This experience of heightened vitality and potency fills me with joy. I experience myself as over-flowing, spending, alive, hence as joyous. Giving is more joyous than receiving, not because it is a deprivation, but because in the act of giving lies the expression of my aliveness.

—Erich Fromm

In the sphere of material things giving means being rich. Not he who has much is rich, but he who gives much. The hoarder who is anxiously worried about losing something is, psychologically speaking, the poor, impoverished man, regardless of how much he has. Whoever is capable of giving of himself is rich.

—Erich Fromm

Be not forgetful to entertain strangers: for thereby some have entertained angels unawares.

—Hebrews: 13:2

No man lives in a vacuum. As each drop of water added to the ocean displaces all the waters of all the seas, the good effort of each man benefits all men; the inefficiencies and errors and evils of each man augment the tribulation of all men.

—CLYDE BEDELL

I expect to pass through life but once. If therefore, there be any kindness I can show, or any good thing I can do to any fellow-being, let me do it now, and not defer or neglect it, as I shall not pass this way again.

WILLIAM PENN

A teacher who can arouse a feeling for one single good action, for one single good poem, accomplishes more than he who fills our memory with rows on rows of natural objects, classified with name and form.

—JOHANN WOLFGANG VON GOETHE

What wisdom can you find that is greater than kindness?

—JEAN JACQUES ROUSSEAU

Anticipate charity by preventing poverty; assist the reduced fellowman, either by a considerable gift, or a sum of money, or by teaching him a trade, or by putting him in the way of business, so that he may earn an honest livelihood, and not be forced to the dreadful alternative of holding out his hand for charity. This is the highest step and the summit of charity's golden ladder.

—MOSES BEN MAIMON
(MAIMONIDES)

A man's true wealth hereafter, is the good he does in this world to his fellow-man. When he dies, people will say, "What property has he left behind him?" But the angels will ask, "What good deeds has he sent before him?"

—MAHOMET

He who allows his day to pass without practicing generosity and enjoying life's pleasures is like a blacksmith's bellows—he breathes but does not live.

—SANSKRIT PROVERB

(85) *Helping Others*

Thou shalt love thy neighbor as thyself.

—Apostle Paul (Romans 13:9, Galatians 5:14, and James 2:8)

Great ideas, it has been said, come into the world as gently as doves. Perhaps, then, if we live attentively, we shall hear, amid the uproar of empires and nations, a faint flutter of wings, the gentle stirring of life and hope. Some will say that this hope lies in a nation; others, in a man. I believe, rather, that it is awakened, revived, nourished by millions of solitary individuals whose deeds and works every day negate frontiers and the crudest implications of history. . . . Each and every man, on the foundations of his own sufferings and joys, builds for all.

—Albert Camus

Treat each man in such a manner that you increase his faith in you and in mankind.

No man needs one of my smiles more than the man who has offered me one of his frowns.

Not all things and actions that might be important or pleasing to us will be important or pleasing to another. Do not do to others simply (as stated by the Golden Rule in Matthew 7:12) "Whatsoever ye would that men should do to you." Rather do, to as great an extent as is feasible, to others what *they* would have you do to them.

❧❧

It is a favor to others if we allow them to do favors for us. By accepting a favor graciously we do a favor!

❧❧

The "meaning" of life is meaningless except in terms of service to others.

❧❧

How can we help make a man happy for the rest of his life? By making him happy *now*—right *now*. He will be happy throughout his life each time he remembers the kindness we have done.

❧❧

If we treat our friends as if they already *are* what they are capable of *becoming*, we help them make the vision into an actuality.

❧❧

If we are being forced to listen to gossip, how can we turn the conversation toward other subjects? A tactful way to achieve this is to listen for a word that may be used to divert the conversation into other channels. If someone says, "She certainly does very little to train her children!" we might select the word "train" and say, "Training children is an interesting subject. I've heard that next to love the most important thing children require is discipline. Do you believe in spanking a child?" If we should have difficulty finding a word on which to turn the conversation, we might simply say, "She's one of the world's finest housekeepers. Everything is always so neat and clean. By the way, have I told you how wonderful my end table looks since I tried using that new American Beauty Wax?"

Here is a conversation diverter we might use if someone starts to gossip about our friend Joe: "Joe's a wonderful bowler. By the way, did I tell you about the 212 game I had last week? Well, I had a rough time for the first two frames, but . . ." Still another conversation diverter we might try is, "Joe's a wonderful gardener. Have you seen his roses? I wonder what kind of rose food he uses."

Whenever we desire to divert a conversation from gossip to another topic let's try, if possible, to select a topic we know is of interest to the other person. But, in any event, our primary object should be to stop the gossip and only secondarily to continue the conversation with a topic the other person will find interesting.

❧❧

In all my associations with others, my primary aims should be to put them at ease and to show them that they are appreciated.

❧❧

How can I encourage a shy person to talk? By appearing to be unfamiliar with, but interested in learning about, a subject on which he is well-informed.

❧❧

Let's work at putting the other fellow at ease by talking about a subject on which he is an expert—*himself*. We might ask about his line of work; ask how he happened to get started in that business; ask where he's from; ask if he has a family; ask about his hobbies. Encourage him to talk of his interest and give him admiration and praise. By helping *him* to overcome *his* inferiority feeling, *his* feeling of shyness, *his* self-consciousness, we'll lose *ours*.

❧❧

We cannot help others without gaining happiness for ourselves. But we derive the greatest happiness when we ignore—yes, even forget this rule of life. The fullest happiness is achieved when we give to others our time, our energy, our smiles, our encouragement and give them for the joy of giving and not for the end of gaining happiness for ourselves. By ignoring the by-product of giving—our own happiness—we achieve the greatest happiness.

In helping others—in giving them our time, our energy, our appreciation—we must not look for their gratitude in return. At times our kindnesses will not be appreciated. If we have a well-developed spirit of tolerance we will accept and be unmoved by the fact that there are men and women who do not habitually express thankfulness. If we looked for a "thank-you" each time we helped others we would be giving not for the joy of giving but for the joy of being thanked. When others thank us for our kindnesses, however, we must, of course, accept their thanks with appreciation. Thus we allow them to experience the happiness that comes from knowing that their gratitude is appreciated.

❦❦

When we leave someone we might ask ourselves, "Does he feel better, or does he feel less happy, for having talked with me?"

❦❦

I must work on the problem of putting at ease those of my associates I excel in certain areas. I must continually stress their superiority in other areas.

I never met a person who did not excel me in many abilities. By discussing, by asking questions, by stressing the importance of the skills at which he excels, I can gain information and further our friendship.

❦❦

Today I am going to cater to the deepest desire of every person I will meet—the desire to be appreciated.

❧❧

When someone comes to us with a serious personal problem, let's listen attentively without interrrupting. Simply allowing him to talk out his problem will help him relax and may show him a solution. We must avoid ridiculing, kidding, laughing, or making light of the problem. Above all, we must not appear to be shocked.

Only after we are certain that we know exactly the true nature of the problem should we offer any advice. Even then, such advice should be in the nature of suggestions. Every person desires to solve his own problems. We perform the greatest service to others, not by solving their problems, but by helping them to understand those problems more clearly so that they themselves may have the satisfaction of discovering their own solutions.

❧❧

Whoever fails to give the gift of himself in the service of others succeeds in giving to himself the gift of unhappiness.

❧❧

Fear, worry, shyness, and lack of confidence are not ours alone but are traits possessed by all men. When we understand ourselves we will understand others. We ought to live and act in such a manner that we will decrease the fear, the worry, the shyness of others and increase their hope, their confidence, their friendliness, and their happiness.

❧❧

Others begin to like us better if, through us, they have first learned to like themselves better.

❧❧

Perhaps very little of the unhappiness of people is caused by evil acts. It is the tactless words, the bitter things said in the course of arguments, that lead to so much unhappiness. Goodness consists not only in the doing of good deeds, but in the saying of kind words.

❧❧

If someone says, "Will you do me a favor?" it's good to say "Yes!" *before* inquiring as to its nature. Let's always be ready and anxious to help.

❧❧

What a great waste is represented by the smiles we failed to give, the friendly words we failed to speak, the love we failed to show! How often we have failed to add to the world's wealth of happiness!

❧❧

Not only try to help those whose inferiority feelings are expressed by shyness but also those whose inferiority feelings are expressed by loudness.

❧❧

You and I have an inexhaustible supply of the things people value most highly—smiles, friendliness, understanding, and appreciation. The more we give away, the more we are enriched.

❧❧

The greatest gifts we can give to others are not material things but gifts of ourselves. The great gifts are those of love, of inspiration, of kindness, of encouragement, of forgiveness, of ideas and ideals. How many great gifts can we give this day?

❧❧

Do we desire to develop our character and to improve our personality? Then let's devote each day of our life to making others happy! A fine character and pleasing personality are formed through dedicating our lives to the service of others.

❧❧

Rainy, cloudy days have a tendency to induce unhappy moods. Let's try, on such days, to be especially cheerful. Smile more; give more compliments. Welcome rainy, cloudy days for these are the days when our efforts to spread smiles and good cheer will be most appreciated.

❧❧

To each person I will meet today I will speak words that will put him at ease—words that say I appreciate him—words that tell him I am his friend.

❧❧

We *like* people for what they can do for us—giving us the pleasure of their company, the joy of corresponding with them, the example of their fine character. We *love* people for what we can do for them.

❧❧

Each day let's do someone a good turn—one that will either *not* be discovered or will be discovered only by accident.

❧❧

Life is a mirror in which the reflection of generous giving is generous receiving.

❧❧

The greatest gift we can give another is to help him to help himself—to inspire him to become the great person he *can* become.

❧

If you or I had been the innkeeper at Bethlehem on one night some two thousand years ago would we have said, "Come in"? Whom have we helped today? Whom have we turned away?

❧

Isn't it possible to foresee a new way of defining "greatness"? Perhaps some day a man's greatness will be measured by the number of persons he has made happy, confident, and less afraid. Your "greatness" and mine may be small—but we can dedicate our lives to increasing it. Let's do what we can to make others happy, confident, and less afraid.

7

Getting Along with People

Civilization is such a good idea that somebody ought to start it.

—Albert Schweitzer

There is something that is much more scarce, something finer far, something rarer than ability. It is the ability to recognize ability.

—Elbert Hubbard

I have never known—really known—a man or woman I couldn't like and respect. I hope I never do. Once we recognize the fact that every individual is a treasury of hidden and unsuspected qualities, our lives become richer, our judgment better, and our world is more right.

This I believe—it is not love that is blind; it is only the unnoticing eye that cannot see the real qualities of man.

—Charles H. Percy

What is true for you in your private heart is true for all men.

—Ralph Waldo Emerson

Do not unto others what you would not have them do unto you.

—CONFUCIUS

We have committed the Golden Rule to memory. Let us now commit it to life.

—EDWIN MARKHAM

Man is to be trained chiefly by studying and by knowing man.

—WILLIAM GLADSTONE

A man is great as a man, be he where or what he may: the grandeur of his nature turns to insignificance all outward distinctions.

—WILLIAM ELLERY CHANNING

The key to a true sense of obligation toward our neighbor lies in the depth and sincerity of our sense of his reality. If he is real to us, if his freedom, his hopes, his nature, his problems, his existence, are really felt and accepted by us as being as real and as important as our own, then, and to that degree, will we feel an obligation toward him in the way we use our freedom.

—STEPHEN F. BAYNE, JR.

When we have a problem getting along with someone, let's analyze *ourselves* and *our* actions. What are *we* doing wrong?

Success and happiness come to those who find it easy to agree with others while disagreeing agreeably with those with whom they cannot agree.

❦❦

Let's start rumors! Tell someone, "I sure like Mary; she's a wonderful person." Tell another, "Jim sure does a fine job of everything he tackles." Use "gossip carriers" to carry sincere compliments back to the persons you've talked about. That's a sure way to make friends!

❦❦

Why not avoid the words "I," "me," and "mine" and substitute the words "you," "your," "we," "our," and "us"? Resolve to talk in terms of the other person's viewpoint and interests.

❦❦

Our greatest wealth consists of the gifts we have given away—smiles, kind words, encouragement to men who frown.

❦❦

Avoid arguments that arise because, unrealized by the arguers, each has a very different definition for a key word. Watch out for discussions involving words like "art," "poetry," "ethics," "democracy," and so forth where an unrealized difference in definitions can lead to an argument.

❦❦

I am going to make it a rule to start each conversation, whenever possible, with a sincere compliment. Some of my compliments I can plan in advance. Before starting out each morning I am going to ask myself:

1. Whom will I see today?
2. What do I admire in each?
3. What words shall I use to express my admiration?

❧❧

After meeting someone let's write his name on an index card for our "friends file" along with notes concerning his appearance to aid us in recognizing him the next time that we meet him. Also record data concerning his family, occupation, hobbies, and so forth as a further aid to conversation when we meet him again.

Another idea is to write down on each of the cards at least three things we admire about that person. Such a practice forces us to seek the good in each person we meet—forces us to be appreciative rather than critical. Thus it can make each of us into a finer person—one whom our acquaintances would like to think of as a friend.

❧❧

A statement containing the word "all," "always," or "never" is usually false. Broad statements are argument-starters and friend-losers.

❧❧

Big favors may breed resentment. Little favors build friendship.

❧❧

How can we make a good impression on others? By letting them know they are making a good impression on us.

❧❧

If there is any kind thing that I can do for or say to someone, I will do or say it *now*. If I have smiles to pass out I will pass them out *now*. Not just tomorrow, but *now*.

❧❧

Make expressions of gratitude just as specific as possible. Instead of saying merely, "Thanks for the book," let's add, "The author paints such wonderful word-pictures." Instead of simply saying, "Thank you for the beautiful letter-opener," go on to say, "It makes such an attractive addition to my desk and greatly speeds up the job of opening the mail."

❧❧

When the words, "I'm sorry to trouble you, but I wonder if you'd mind . . ." precede a request, that request will be granted, not grudgingly, but enthusiastically!

❧❧

When a man is wrong he may admit it to himself. He may even take pride in admitting it to others. But if we try to convince him of his error, and do it in a manner which he feels reflects on his judgment or intelligence, he will defend his position stubbornly and vociferously.

To convince a man that he is in error we must begin by seeming to agree with his position. Using the Ben Franklin technique, we may observe that in many cases and circumstances his opinion would be correct but that in the present case there appears to be some difference. Let's ask questions in a friendly manner—questions that will get a "yes" response—questions that will eventually permit him to discover for himself that he is wrong.

❧❧

Be careful that the voice does not convey an unfriendly feeling. Kind words, to be effective, should be accompanied by smiles and a friendly tone of voice.

❧❧

When someone complains about something we have done or have failed to do, thank him for bringing the matter to our attention. We should tell him that he has done us a great favor for, if what we have done or have failed to do has annoyed him, it has probably annoyed others also and, unknown to us, it may be causing a loss of friends. We ought to tell him we appreciate having the opportunity to correct the condition.

❦❦

What are the other person's dominant interests? Are they his family, money-making, reading, woodworking, stamp collecting, travel? I will discover these interests. The way I think, speak, and act will show that I feel they are important.

❦❦

How can I most easily achieve my goals? By closely relating my objectives to the interests of those who can help me.

❦❦

To be good conversationalists we must be good listeners. When we listen, let's not look out the window, write, light a cigarette, or shuffle papers. Instead, we should look at the speaker and concentrate on his words rather than on what we are going to say in reply. Through careful listening we pay a silent compliment to the speaker; we tell him that what he has to say is important and interesting to us.

❦❦

Don't you think it is worth some effort to remember names of persons we meet? The way the memory experts do it is to associate the person and his name with some picture. If we are introduced to a bit-too-plump Miss Slowonski, let's picture her on skis and making very little progress. She's so plump that she's slow . . . on . . . skis. When we meet a Mr. Heiby we might picture him riding on a huge bee that is buzzing around the top of the Empire State Building (a high bee). Preferably, we should make our picture a ridiculous one. That will insure its being more memorable. One word of warning—frequently our pictures will be somewhat insulting and so they should be kept secret.

To insure that we will remember the name of the person to whom we have just been introduced, it is best to keep using his name frequently in our conversation: "Are you a native of Chicago, Mr. Dorsey?" or "What is your line of work, Mr. Dorsey?"

Similarly, we want to be sure that he remembers our name. Therefore, we look for an opportunity to repeat our own name. We might say, for example, "He said to me, 'Mr. Heiby, we've got the best corn crop that we've had in ten years.' "

If we have any doubt as to the correct pronunciation of a name we might simply ask, "Am I pronouncing your name properly?" If the name is difficult we should say, "I'm sorry, would you mind spelling it?" Our new acquaintance will be pleased that we are enough interested in him to feel that his name is important. His own name is a more interesting topic of conversation for him than are idle observations about the weather.

Showing gratitude extends beyond a mere expression of "Thanks" or "You're welcome"—the usual way of showing our gratitude for someone else's gratitude. Instead of "You're welcome," why not say, "It's nice to be nice to nice people." When someone gives us a compliment, instead of saying, "Thank you," we might reply, "You always say and do such nice things." When the boss compliments us for doing a good job we might reply, "Working for you is a real pleasure."

If we are being thanked for having helped someone, a friendly reply might be, "It's the least I could do to say 'thank you' for all the help you've given me" (or ". . . for all the fine things you've done for me.") If a customer admires an innovation we have introduced we might say, "If *you* like it—*we* like it." If we are being thanked by guests for a pleasant evening we might say,

"Thank *you* for coming. It's always so nice to have you with us." Let's continually think up more friendly ways of saying "Thank you" and "You're welcome."

❧❧

We make others feel inferior when we overexplain everything we say. Such overexplaining implies that the other person is stupid. Isn't it better to make others feel superior by making explanations at a level that assumes they are superior?

❧❧

Compliments are most powerful when they are specific. To praise a meal is far more effective if we admire specifically the sweet potatoes or the fresh corn. But we should try to admire the items where the cook used her skill. Let's not praise the thousand island dressing that came out of a jar which was bought at the store, but rather admire the apple pie that required considerable skill for its preparation.

❧❧

Whenever two persons have a difference of opinion, an effort should be made to avoid misunderstandings that can lead to an argument. Upon discovering such a difference of opinion we might make it a rule to state the other's position. Such words as "You mean to say that . . ." or "Do I understand that your opinion is . . ."—such words will clear the way for understanding. When there is understanding, a spirit of discussion rather than one of argument will prevail.

❧❧

Let's be careful of the mental associations that we put into words. If you are looking at a horror show, don't ask your wife when her mother is coming for a visit. If a friend parks his car badly we should not talk about the careless driving we witnessed this morning. If you see a steam shovel gobbling up tons of dirt, don't ask your wife if her brother is coming for dinner tonight. If I'm looking at a friend's garden, I must avoid talking about the ragweed that grows near my home. It is important to edit our associations before we voice them!

❧❧

When someone tells me a joke I have heard before or tells me about a new scientific development or a piece of business news, I will try to refrain from saying, "I've heard that one before" or "I read about that in the morning newspaper." I will let the other person display his talent and his information.

❧❧

A man appreciates a compliment regarding a trait or an activity at which he *desires* to excel more than a compliment about something in which he obviously already excels. If we listen carefully as he talks we can discover his desires. Then, by complimenting him in ways relating to these aspirations, we will have gained a friend.

❧❧

If someone makes an insulting remark to us we might look directly into his eyes and remain silent a moment—then smile. Let's say, "Would you mind repeating that? I'm not sure I understood you." As he repeats his insult, the chances are that he will begin to see the foolishness of his remark. An apology is the probable result.

❧❧

To gain and keep a man's attention, let's talk in terms of his interest and his experience.

❦

Here is a five-point program for calming another man's anger:

1. Listen silently while he angrily recites his grievances.
2. When he has finished, and we are sure he has finished, look at him expectantly as if we believe he has even more to say.
3. After several seconds of complete silence say, "Would you please go over the problem again? I want to make sure that I understand exactly what the difficulty is." As he proceeds to repeat his story his anger will have diminished considerably and he is even likely to apologize for being unreasonable. The cardinal rule is to meet his anger with silence; let *him* do the talking.
4. After he has finished the second telling of his story ask him, in a series of requests, to explain several of the points he has just mentioned. Through this questioning procedure we will not only get all the facts but he will clarify his own thinking—which is apt to be anything but clear when he is angry.
5. His anger has disappeared. An intelligent discussion can now proceed and lead to a solution of the problem.

❦

In writing or in conversation, let's try to match each of our "*I's*" with two or more "*you's*".

❦

A good conversationalist is one who succeeds in his purpose of pleasing the persons with whom he is talking.

❦

My father, who taught mathematics during most of his professional lifetime, acted for a brief period as principal of a school in South

Dakota. On frequent occasions teachers would present problems and ask for his advice. Recognizing that the teachers were frequently in a better position than he to reach a decision he would ask, "How would *you* solve this problem?" or "What do *you* recommend?" Following this procedure he was not only able to help guide the teachers to a good solution but, because he showed that he appreciated their ideas, he was able to gain their loyalty and cooperation.

❧❧

To be a good conversationalist one must be a good listener. To become a good listener one must develop a desire to understand and appreciate the other man's viewpoint. Be sure you understand his motives as well as his words because frequently words can be misleading. Remember that no matter what his words say, it must be taken as axiomatic that people do not deliberately try to be offensive. Look beyond the words in order to see the motives—and you will find that the motives are good.

Good conversation requires that our replies to another's words be made not only with an understanding of his words but of his viewpoint and of his motives. Silence is a better reply than words that demonstrate a lack of appreciation.

❧❧

A compliment should be gracefully accepted, not denied. To deny a compliment would imply that the compliment giver is a liar.

❧❧

When your wife asks whether you would prefer creamed corn or green beans for dinner, tell her your choice. Leaving the decision up to her, in order to let her choose whichever *she* prefers, is being considerate but in a restricted sense. You are forcing her to make a decision which may be more painful to her than eating beans when she would prefer corn. When asked to make a decision, make it!

How do we avoid an argument? By stressing repeatedly the things on which we agree. By emphasizing that we are both working toward the same goal but differ only in our opinion of the way in which it can best be achieved.

To avoid arguments, shun the use of words that start arguments—words that express finality. Examples of such words are "Completely!" "Always!" "Invariably!" "Never!" If a man expresses an opinion and we counter with one of these blood-boiling words, the fight is on! When we feel compelled to disagree with a statement it is better to use, instead, a friendly approach such as, "That may be right in many cases, but in this instance it appears to me . . . ," or "I'm sure that much could be said for that viewpoint, but it's my opinion that, in this particular case . . ."

A good listener earns the reputation for being a good conversationalist. Let's listen without interrupting until the other person finishes. If we have something important to say, it is best to wait until the other man has made his point so that he will have a free mind to listen carefully to us.

What is the basic formula for starting a conversation with a stranger? Give him a compliment or ask him for information or for advice.

When we hear a person being praised, let's add to the praises rather than countering with complaints. The scientist's method of fully stating both pros and cons does not belong in the repertory of good human relations.

Let's be careful that we do not unwittingly write insulting letters. If a prospect asks for a quotation we should not tell him, "You failed to specify the models you desire." Imagine how we would feel if the boss said, "You failed to write this quotation in a friendly manner." We would feel better if the boss said, "I failed to explain to you how I want quotations handled." We might apply the same treatment to our prospect and say, "We're not sure just which models you're interested in but will be happy to quote on your exact requirements if you just tell us your wishes." In this way, we are telling the prospect there is something *we* don't know and not blaming *him* for a failure.

There are many many phrases that make others unhappy, for example "You claim that," "According to you," "You overlooked sending," "You are hereby notified," "You do not understand," "You are probably ignorant of this fact," or "You made an error." Just as bad are such expressions as "It is not possible for me to," "I have not had the courtesy of a reply," or "We have been very patient." Especially bad are words that command. In place of "We ask that you," we might substitute "May we have." Instead of "You ought to," substitute "Perhaps you could." We should avoid also, as far as possible, use of such negative words as "problem," "trouble," and "complaint."

And, speaking of "complaints," let's welcome a complaint letter from a customer. It presents a wonderful opportunity to show him that he is dealing with a company that believes in customer satisfaction. Properly handled, a "complaint" can produce a lifelong customer-friend.

❧❧

If you're so smart why can't you get others to think you are modest?

❧❧

When we attempt to fix the blame for an error, we succeed only in developing a spirit of enmity and of non-cooperation. Instead of dwelling on the subject of who was to blame, it is better to spend our energies in finding ways to avoid future mistakes. Furthermore, let's do it in a spirit of helpfulness, of patience, and of understanding.

❧❧

No one needs help with his own human relations more than the man who despises the subject or its study.

❧❧

You say that someone has condemned you for saying something or doing something because he misinterpreted your words or actions? Then should you ever condemn another for his words or actions without making an exhaustive study to determine every possible meaning those words and actions might have been meant to convey? Condemnation is easy; understanding is not.

❧❧

It's wise, at times, to appear to be otherwise.

❧❧

If we can quote to a man the words that he said to us on a former occasion we will thereby pay him a much-appreciated compliment.

We will have thus succeeded in telling him that we listened to him carefully and his words were so meaningful that we committed them to memory.

❦❦

When you are asked for your opinion there is *always* something pleasant that can be said that is, at the same time, true. Think, determine what it is, and then answer.

❦❦

There is a formula for becoming friendly with even a most difficult person. *Find one thing upon which you can both agree and forget the things on which you disagree.*

❦❦

Do you think two persons would argue if each thought of the argument as being an episode about which he would later tell another, relating it as an amusing anecdote?

❦❦

His attitude will be improved when you improve yours.

❦❦

When the conversation turns to such emotional and controversial topics as politics or religion, it may not be wise to state our opinions directly. Instead, we might try introducing our ideas indirectly with a phrase such as "Some people believe that . . . ," or "Don't you think it's conceivable that . . . ?" When a temper-stimulating topic is the subject of conversation, it is sometimes best to restrain ourselves from bluntly expressing our ideas when to do so would gain us nothing but enemies.

Certain comparisons tend to poison human relations. The remark, "This is the finest cake I've ever tasted," insults the baking talents of the other women who are either present or who may later hear about your comment. Merely saying, "This is a wonderful cake," keeps us out of trouble and is equally complimentary. Let's not say, "She's the best president our P.T.A. ever had," since that will tend to humiliate all previous P.T.A. presidents to whom the statement may be repeated. Isn't the observation, "She's a fine president," just as satisfactory? Comparisons are necessary in the field of science, in marketing analysis, and in many other situations, but they are a threat to successful human relations. Let's avoid such comparisons!

Upon being introduced to someone, there are words we can use that are far more friendly than "How do you do?" "How are you?" or "I'm pleased to meet you." Our new acquaintance will more likely be pleasantly impressed with us if we say, "I've often heard of you, Mr. Smith," providing we can say this honestly. "This is a *real* pleasure, Mr. Jones" can always be used and is effective in creating friendliness. Perhaps the best words of all to use upon being introduced to Mr. Brown by your friend Jim are, "Jim has often mentioned you, Mr. Brown." These are words that compliment both Jim and Mr. Brown and so they are doubly effective as friend-builders.

If you must discuss a subject that might lead to disagreements, do it, whenever possible, on a sunny, not-too-hot day. When the day is cloudy or the temperature is above 90 degrees, it is difficult for one to consider a problem in a fair and pleasant manner. On sunless days the atmospheric pressure is likely to be low—another factor tending to shorten tempers. It is equally difficult on a cloudy day for the person to whom a problem is being presented to react in a fair and pleasant manner. Cloudy and/or hot days breed arguments. Clear, cool days of high atmospheric pressure bring easy agreement.

❧❧

Next time we hear someone mispronounce a word, let's mispronounce it ourselves if we must use it immediately in talking with that person. Unless he is paying us as a tutor, or we are a parent correcting our child, or there might be a danger in failing to make the correction, why should we insult someone by correcting him?

❧❧

Give praise generously where it is deserved, but be sincere in that praise. It is better to tell a woman, "You have such lovely hair" and mean it, than to say, "You are the prettiest girl in the world," when she knows, and she feels you know, that the statement is false.

It is better to praise activities or attributes rather than the person, himself. Praise a man for what he *does* or *has,* not for what he *is.* Say "You sure know how to throw a bowling ball," rather than "You're the finest bowler in this league." Say "Your typing is beautiful," not "You're a fine typist." When we praise someone for what he does or has we are being specific and therefore we sound more sincere.

Let's be generous with our compliments and give them whenever we can do so sincerely. When we help someone to like himself better, we cause him to like us.

❧❧

The surest way of making a good impression is to let the other person know that we are impressed by him. When complimenting a person, preferably select a virtue that is not completely obvious. A man with the muscles of Atlas knows he is strong and does not find constant recognition of his strength particularly satisfying. Praise him for the birdhouse he has built and he will glow with pride.

Make the other person feel important. The way to get across to others the idea that we think they are wonderful is to remind ourselves continually that *people are important.*

❧❧

Let's avoid teasing and kidding. These are the great destroyers of the victim's self-esteem and should be avoided. Even close friends, while accepting kidding in a gracious manner, do not like it.

❧❧

It is well-established that egotistical persons have not too much appreciation for themselves, but too little. The person who likes himself gets along well with others. The sensitive person, who interprets the most innocent remark as being an insult to himself, is suffering from a tremendous lack of self-esteem. The loud ones, those arrogant persons who like to make others feel inferior, also have a poor opinion of themselves and hope that this voluble offensiveness will add to their self-importance.

It's wrong to add to the troubles of such persons by arguing with them for if we did "win" the arguments we would surely cause them further loss of self-esteem. Rather, we should find things to compliment and help them to evaluate more generously their own talents. Thus, we will have helped them to overcome their inferiority complex and become likeable persons. Let's help people to like themselves better!

F. Assume the stranger will be friendly and begin your conversation in a friendly manner by asking questions about his ideas, work, and hobbies. Or we might try starting with a comment relating to one of these:
   1. News. (Read two papers daily. Do not neglect editorials, book reviews, movie criticism.)
   2. Ads in newspapers, magazines, buses. (Watch for language oddities.)
   3. Your surroundings. (Comment on the furniture, paintings, garden.)
   4. Transportation. (How you got to where you are.)

❧❧

In virtually every conversation we are presented with numerous opportunities to benefit from a display of silence.

❧❧

Good human relations are fostered with Mr. and Mrs. Jones by making certain we never quite keep up with the Joneses.

❧❧

Each man I will meet today is in some way far superior to me. How can I let each know indirectly, so I will not be suspected of flattery, that I recognize his superiority?

8

Friendship

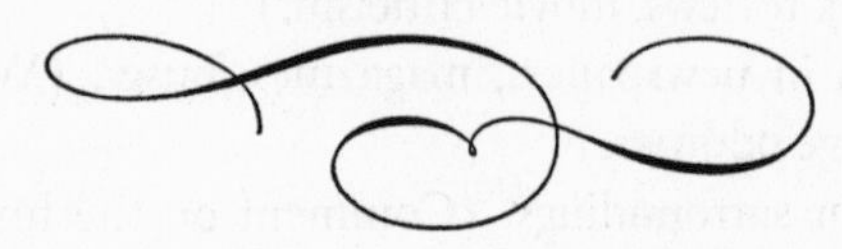

The person who is most likely to make you a good friend or business associate is one who is already making a success of living in his other relationships; who has wholesome attitudes toward himself as a member of one sex, and feels friendly, rather than hostile or suspicious, toward the opposite sex; who gets along well in his marital and parental relationships; who enjoys, or at least does not dislike, his work; and who finds that living is fun. But in the final analysis, the best basis of judgment is his record.

—Sylvanus M. Duvall

But who shall say that Jesus, loving the woman caught in adultery, did not also include in that love each of all those who came to stone her to death, and by his inclusive love shielded them all from murder.

—Robert Raynolds

Brotherly love is love for all human beings; it is characterized by its very lack of exclusiveness. If I have developed the capacity for love, then I cannot help loving my brothers. In brotherly love there is the experience of union with all men, of human solidarity, of human at-onement. Brotherly love is based on the experience that we all are one. The differences in talents, intelligence, knowledge are negligible in comparison with the identity of the human core common to all men. In order to experience this identity it is necessary to penetrate from the periphery to the core. If I perceive in another person mainly the surface, I perceive mainly the differences, that which separates us. If I penetrate to the core, I perceive our identity, the fact of our brotherhood.

—Erich Fromm

. . . what if our love for one differs from our love for another? Is it therefore not love?

—Robert Raynolds

That friendship will not continue to the end which is begun for an end.

—Francis Quarles

The only way to have a friend is to be one.

—Ralph Waldo Emerson

He drew a circle that shut me out—
Heretic, rebel, a thing to flout.
But Love and I had the wit to win:
We drew a circle that took him in!

—Edwin Markham

My People? Who are they?
I went into the church where the congregation
Worshiped my God. Were they my people?
I felt no kinship to them as they knelt there.
My People! Where are they?
I went into the land where I was born,
Where men spoke my language . . .
I was a stranger there.
"My people," my soul cried. "Who are my people?"

Last night in the rain I met an old man
Who spoke a language I do not speak,
Which marked him as one who does not know my God.

With apologetic smile he offered me
The shelter of his patched umbrella.
I met his eyes . . . And then I knew . . .

—Rosa Zagnoni Marinoni

Place a penny on a table. Move it a few inches. It is no longer the same penny—it is a similar penny. It has grown older. It now has a slightly different temperature since different places in a room always vary somewhat in temperature. New dust particles and different air molecules now cling to its surface. Other magnetic lines of force and radio waves are now passing through it. It lost a few molecules of copper and so lost some weight through friction when it was moved.

You and I are not the same persons we were yesterday. Experience has changed some of our attitudes. Today's sunshine as opposed to yesterday's cloudiness, has changed other attitudes. The man who may have displeased us yesterday is not the same person today. Perhaps he is a friend.

❦❦

A friendly person shows friendship to others not because *they* are friendly but because *he* is friendly.

❦❦

Those who have hurt me, I will forgive. But forgiveness is not enough. I will wish them every good thing in life. I will believe that good will is contagious and that they can be my friends.

❦❦

Suppose we have met someone for the first time just ten minutes ago. He is a person we would like to know much better but now, after exchanging thoughts rather briefly, we must break away. What can we say to him that will make him want to know us better? Along with our "good-bys" we might say this: "I've known you for just a short time but I think you're a very interesting person. Let's really make it a point to get together again soon."

Let's make a new friend today!

Many, many of the persons *we* fear are just as afraid of *us*. They are afraid that we will not approve of them just as we fear they will not approve of us. Let's start a conversation with a stranger today. We can make observations or ask questions about the weather or our surroundings. Better yet, we might ask him to do us a small favor. Ask the time, or ask directions to a prominent landmark that he is virtually certain to know about. Nothing makes friends faster than a favor generously granted because it makes both persons feel good. Of course, the favor asked must be small enough to be readily granted or the technique is doomed to failure.

Leaders take the lead in getting to know others. Next time you are in a large meeting observe who is most active in introducing himself to strangers. It is the important, the enthusiastic, the really-alive man, isn't it? He is a man who has actively worked at extending his circle of friends until it has become spontaneous with him. He could be you. He could be me.

When passing a friend on the street, instead of reciting the usual "Good morning," "Hi!" "Hello," "How's it going?" why not, for a change, simply smile and enthusiastically say "Howard!" If not on a first-name basis, let's accompany our big smile with an enthusiastic, "Mr. Taylor!"

❧

When someone does you a favor don't be too quick to favor him in return. Isn't it more thoughtful to allow him, for a few days, to enjoy the luxury of your being obligated?

❧

I'll telephone a friend today. Perhaps I'll invite him to lunch. Or I'll write him a note just to tell him I'm glad he's my friend.

Wouldn't it be wise to avoid the excessive busyness that keeps us from our friends?

❧

Let's write more letters we don't have to write—letters of congratulations—letters that just say, "I'm glad I've got you for a friend."

Resolve to show appreciation of others and of their accomplishments by writing those letters we don't have to write!

❧

We like those who like us. Those we like find it easy to like us. "Likingness" is circular. Make the first move to form a new circle of "likingness."

❧

Any man whose viewpoint I understand is a potential friend.

❧

When we feel misunderstood by others we should examine ourselves. What negative attitude of our own is inhibiting a friendly relationship?

❧

Through repartee we tend to develop another's envy. Through admiration for his repartee we develop friendship.

Love has more power to unite the world than the hydrogen bomb to destroy it.

If I would make a new friend today and every day and you would make a new friend today and every day and each of our new friends would make a new friend today and every day, could there ever be another war?

We learn to like others by thinking about their admirable qualities and by avoiding a continual inventory-taking of their characteristics that we do not like.

Think of a person whose friendship or cooperation you desire. What talent or accomplishment of his can you praise? In front of whom would he especially like being praised?

Love of mankind is an empty phrase unless we can first learn to love our neighbor.

It is friendly to say "thanks" for a gift later as well as at the time it is received. Thanking someone who has given us a book, not only at the time it is received, but also after we have read it, is a very gracious act. Another "Thank you" given later—when not called for by etiquette—is the most effective and most appreciated.

The strength of friendship and love is measured by the desire to share the silences as well as the words.

It is better to lose the argument and gain a friend than to win the argument and lose a friend.

Here is a way we can let others know we are thinking of them. When we read an article in a newspaper or magazine that we think might interest one of our friends or acquaintances let's clip it out, write on the margin, "Thought you might not have read this," sign, and mail it. This idea is subject to almost infinite expansion if we work at it. We can clip articles relating to topics that were just casually mentioned by our friend in a recent conversation even if such topics don't relate to one of his major interests. The thoughtfulness and interest in others that such a project shows can gain friends for us.

We should try our best to understand the other person's viewpoint. Only if we are able to look at a problem as seen *through his eyes* can we hope to get or keep him as a friend. We might ask ourselves, "How would I feel, how would I act, if I were my friend?"

We must be careful in showing off our knowledge or the person to whom we are speaking may feel inferior. On the other hand, there is a great deal to be said for appearing to be ignorant. When we tell others how clumsy we are with tools, how slowly we read, how many mistakes we have made, they love us! To gain friends let's admit to being their inferior in those areas in which we truly are inferior and play down our knowledge and skills in the areas in which we are superior.

❦

Try to find common bonds with others. If someone says that he has recently returned from a visit to New Orleans and it happens that we were there a few years ago, let's be sure to tell him how much we enjoyed eating Oysters Rockefeller at Antoine's, seeing the art show in Pirates Alley, and browsing through the antique shops of Royal Street. If someone says he loves angel food cake and we do, too, we should tell him so. Establishing common bonds with the other person tells him that we are like him. Common bonds develop the bond of friendship.

❦

Most of us discover, sooner or later, that people are not any harder to get along with in one town than another, in one office than another, in one factory than another. We learn, eventually, that the friendliness of others is determined by our own attitudes toward them. Our smiles in any town, in any office, in any factory will bring smiles in return.

❦

Almost everyone desires friendship just as we do. A man, however, is often afraid to appear friendly because he fears that we will reject him. To one who is afraid to be friendly this rejection would be a severe blow to his already suffering ego and so to protect his feelings he assumes a reserved, aloof, unfriendly attitude.

Let's not wait for a friendly sign from persons we meet. Instead, we ought to take the initiative in being friendly. Believe our new acquaintance is going to like us and act as if he will like us. *And he will!*

❦

A smile is the key to the hearts of people. A smile communicates with men of all languages. With a smile we say, "I like you," to an Arab, to a Mongolian, or to one of the Watusi. With a smile we say, "I want to be friendly." Smile more often. Smiles exchanged make a conversation.

❦❦

It is better to give than to receive (including the giving of the gift of happiness that comes when we let someone do something *for us*). Let's *become* obligated to our friends by asking a favor. If we let them do us a favor they will like us even better, as they exercise the feeling that *it is better to give than to receive.*

❦❦

Each time we meet someone, we could promote good human relations by saying to ourselves, "I want to like you." This would automatically encourage us to attempt to discover his admirable qualities. Let's not allow our self-centeredness to keep us from making this stranger into a friend.

❦❦

A stranger is a friend who does not know us.

❦❦

We can't *act* friendly toward someone for very long without *feeling* friendly. If *we* feel friendly, *he'll* feel friendly.

❦❦

Few of us can say with Will Rogers, "I never met a man I didn't like." All of us, however, can say, "I'll never meet a man again that I won't *try* to like."

9

Influencing Others

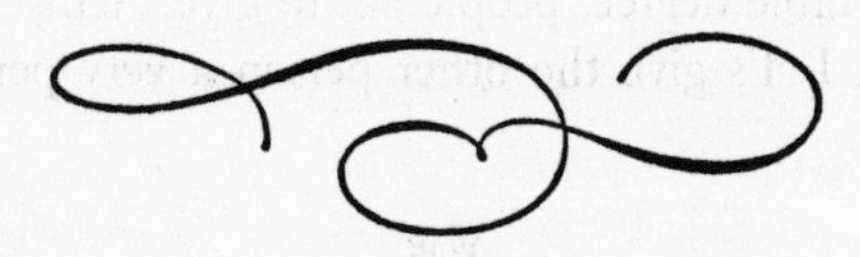

A man without a smiling face must not open a shop.

—Chinese proverb

Men must be taught as if you taught them not
And things unknown proposed as things forgot.

—Alexander Pope

Business is a transaction in which both parties gain.

—Unknown

To know how to suggest is the art of teaching.

—Henri-Frédéric Amiel

Many of us think of salesmen as people traveling around with sample kits. Instead, we are all salesmen, every day of our lives. We are selling our ideas, our plans, our energies, our enthusiasm to those with whom we come in contact.

—Charles M. Schwab

To a considerable degree, people act to give themselves a feeling of importance. Let's give the other person a very personal reason for helping us.

❧❧

Quiet friendliness will often win where loud logic has failed.

❧❧

If I say to a person "I need you" and mean it and convince him that I mean it, I will move him to do my desire.

❧❧

Next time you are caught for a traffic violation, next time you blunder and are found out by your wife, the boss, or a customer, readily admit your error. Say, "I'm guilty. I have no excuses. I'm absolutely wrong. I should know better. This is a serious mistake that I've made. I should have been more careful." Quickly say all the negative things about those actions that the other person is apt to be thinking and do it before *he* has a chance to express *his* thoughts.

Here is what will happen. The other person will assume a magnanimous attitude and will start defending you. He will say, "It's not a bad error. Anyone could have done this. It's really nothing." The other person wants to feel important. He desires to display his generosity. To do this he must defend you. *Self-criticism is a powerful technique for making our mistakes look minor to others.*

The salesman who visualizes each prospect as a friend who will be grateful for having been told about his product or service will sell and sell and sell.

How can we win over someone who disagrees with us? While he is speaking, even though he is expounding thoughts with which we disagree, let's listen attentively and nod our head sympathetically. When it is our turn to present the contrary view, we are apt to find that he will be sympathetic, in turn, to our statements and more likely to be swayed to our way of thinking. After he has made a full explanation, we should agree with him. Say something like this: "I'm sure that if I were you I'd feel exactly the same way you do. From your point of view I'm sure you're absolutely right, but I wonder if there isn't another way of looking at it. The way I see it is this, . . ." Or we could tell him, "There's certainly a lot to be said for your viewpoint. I believe I understand exactly why you feel as you do. But I wonder if you might not agree with some of my thinking. May I have your opinion of this idea?"

In any argumentative situation it is best to quickly agree with your opponent. Agreement keeps the conversation friendly and increases the probability that your words will be convincing.

There is a problem faced continually by salesmen and by all of us on less frequent occasions. It is the problem of gaining the attention of someone with whom we have no appointment so that he listens sympathetically to our story.

An effective way in which to solve this problem is to say, "I have not come to talk to you now, Mr. Jones. I've come simply to find out when you can give me two minutes to answer a question."

Mr. Jones will reply something like this, "I think I can give you two minutes right now. What's your question?" To this invitation we reply, "Would this afternoon or tomorrow be more convenient for you to discuss a radically new method for solving your record storage problems?" Using this technique we have tried for both an immediate presentation and for a definite appointment by mentioning this afternoon and tomorrow. Furthermore, we've done so in a manner that should keep our prospect friendly and receptive.

❧

Whenever I desire someone to do something for me, I am not only going to tell him *what* I would like done but also *when* I would like it done, *how* I would like it done, and *why* I wish it done. The "when," "how," and "why" of the job—not just the "what" of it—develop enthusiasm and cooperation and assure that the job will be finished promptly and properly.

❧

If I am writing an advertisement or a letter or if I am talking directly to a man or group of men and my object is to persuade them to buy, to think, to fight or to take any other action, I must present benefits. My presentation will be effective only if I write or speak in terms of benefits to the other person.

❧

Convincing a man about a new idea is easier if we compliment him by saying, "Here's an idea I'm sure you've known about for years, but perhaps it may have slipped your mind."

❧

How do we get others to agree with us—to agree with us whether we are attempting to sell them a product or to convince them of an idea? The powerful formula is, "Don't ask *if*—ask *which*." The idea is to give others a choice between two products or two courses of action, where the acceptance of either would please us.

A salesgirl who says, "Do you like one of these ties?" will sell less merchandise than one who says, "Which do you prefer—this maroon one or the blue one?" A salesman will arrange more appointments if he says, "Would Tuesday or Friday be more convenient for you?" than if he merely says, "May I come out to see you?"

Back in the Big Depression the Walgreen Drug Stores sold a lot of eggs by using a suggestion of that great "Sell the sizzle—not the steak" salesman and sales trainer, Elmer Wheeler. When a customer ordered a malted milk the clerks had been asking something such as, "Want an egg in your malt, sir?" Wheeler suggested that the clerk hold an egg in each hand and say, "One or two eggs in your malt, sir?"—a question which could not elicit a "no" reply since a "no" would be meaningless. And eggs were sold in great quantity.

Instead of a wife asking her husband, "Shall we eat out some night this week?" her chances of dining out will be greatly increased by her asking, "Shall we have supper in a restaurant Wednesday or Sunday?" Her husband is more apt to get a favorable reply if he asks, "Would Monday or Thursday be more convenient for me to play poker with the boys?"

When we offer a choice the other person has an opportunity to give us his opinion—something all of us love to give. We like and cooperate with the person who lets us express our opinion. Don't ask *if*—ask *which*.

❧❧

The story is told about two shoe salesmen assigned to different areas in underdeveloped regions of Africa. The one wired his home office: "This is a terrible territory. No one here wears shoes." The other sent his boss this message: "This is a wonderful territory. Everyone here needs shoes!"

Which man are you?

❦

Have I a suggestion to give my wife? Have I an idea I'd like to tell the boss? Then I'll phrase them in the form of questions. Questions induce others to cooperate. Questions allow others to talk themselves into the ideas we are promoting.

❦

When you want someone to do a certain thing, encourage him to talk so you have an opportunity to find out his objectives, thus enabling you to determine why he might want to do it. Then try to point out this reason to him as indirectly as possible. You will be more likely to obtain the desired action if he thinks it is his own idea. The way to get a person to do something is to make him *want* to do it!

A great leader induces men, through indirection, to accomplish his end. And, when the project is completed, the follower says, "I did this myself."

❦

The salesman who visualizes himself as one who confers benefits rather than one who merely sells products or services is anxious to help as many people as possible. To do so he wants to make as many calls as possible.

❦

Never tell anyone, "I'm going to prove this fact to you." To do so puts the other man in an inferior position. It implies we are about to demonstrate that we are much smarter than he is. And so we attempt to convince a mind that is closed to whatever we say.

How much better to demonstrate the disputed fact, indirectly, through asking questions! By examining the facts and through implying that we may be wrong, we can permit the other man to convince himself. In this way we gain an enthusiastic supporter for our ideas!

❧❧

To get cooperation in a project, inspire the other person to want to cooperate by giving him a reason for doing so. When a man really *wants* something he will work with unlimited energy to achieve it.

❧❧

Many favors that might not otherwise be granted will be conferred if we ask for them, not in terms of a service to ourselves, but as a benefit to a third person.

❧❧

If you would like to give the impression of knowing your business, make whatever you do look easy to do.

❧❧

When we are forced to give negative criticism of someone's work, let's proceed with great care. We should start with praise for all the good elements we can find. Then we might ask, "Is this the way to handle this particular situation?" Or "There are many problems that would undoubtedly be solved beautifully with your method, but is it the best approach to use with this specific project?" When we must criticize it is best to begin by showing appreciation and then, as indirectly as possible, point out the mistakes that we believe have been made.

❧

If a man becomes angry about something we have done or something we have sold him, we should listen while he talks and talks. After he has finished with his story let's look at the problem from *his point of view*. We will be able to find areas of agreement, admit we are in the wrong, and tell him that if we were he we'd feel just as he does. Then we can say we are sorry to have caused him all this inconvenience, and ask him what he would like us to do. We might go on to thank him for bringing this problem to our attention. Tell him that he has done us a great favor. Say we are probably guilty of offending others just as we did him and only through his thoughtfulness in telling us about it are we able to correct the condition. Probabilities are he will become agreeable and end up trying very hard to be friendly with us.

❧

If we are faced with the problem of answering a complaint letter, let's find something in the letter with which we can agree and begin our letter with the words, "You're absolutely right!" After a start like that he will be agreeable and willing to listen to our side of the story. In this way we can save our company from going broke through a too generous granting of unreasonable requests and at the same time save the good will of a customer.

❧

How can I impress others? By letting them impress me.

❧

If during an argument, or during a discussion that could become an argument, you are tempted to make a loud positive statement contradicting something your opponent has said, substitute a quiet question. Your opponent's viewpoint can be more effectively condemned by his own words than by yours. Loud words do not convince; quiet questions may.

The word "impossible" often functions as an action-stimulator when it is said to a man who likes to get things done.

The salesman who starts out to do a good turn for a prospective customer and who continually, throughout his sales presentation, concentrates on meeting a need and performing a required service, will outsell many times the salesman who concentrates on the problem of moving goods.

If we can get a man to say "yes" to a little thing, it is easier to get a "yes" from him on a big thing.

Don't say to a man, "I know you won't cheat me," but rather, "I know that I can trust you." Let's not, inadvertently, suggest the very thought or action that we are trying to avoid.

If someone gives us a promise, the best insurance that he will actually perform is to announce his promise in public. Disclosing plans to others assures that strenuous effort will be made to carry the project to completion.

When we deal with someone whose nature it is to be contrary, we may find that the usually-unproductive negative approach is useful. If we say, "You wouldn't like to do this, would you?" such a person will probably reply, "And why wouldn't I like to do that?" We should use this negative approach infrequently and do so only after considerable thought. Most persons, happily, react more readily to positive suggestions.

❦❦

Here are some magic words to get others to cooperate with us. They are "we," "us," and "our." It is advisable to use these words frequently when trying to convince others to join us in a given project. Let's put the other person on our team by asking him for his advice, ideas, and opinions on how we can achieve our objective.

❦❦

When trying to convince someone, present the facts and your opinions without exaggeration. Then use the Ben Franklin technique of scratching the head, shaking it a little, and admitting that it is quite possible you may be mistaken. By expressing doubt about our opinions and ideas we frequently put the other person on our side. He tries to convince us that we are right!

❦❦

To gain cooperation, offer a challenge. For example, say, "This is a tough job. It will take a big man to succeed at it."

❦❦

Use charts to stimulate men to greater action. Post a chart showing the number of bags of popcorn each packer has packed so far today, the number of dollars each volunteer has collected thus far in the Red Cross campaign, the number of orders each salesman has obtained, and so forth. A public record is a tremendous stimulus for greater activity. Every person likes to prove he can excel. If we want a man to extend himself, let's give him a challenge!

❦

It is easier to express criticism of someone's actions if we can blame ourselves for the same or similar faults. If we must criticize a girl's typing we might say, "I can't type. I can't even write legibly and I misspell a word or two in every paragraph. I am guilty of so many mistakes that I really have no right to criticize anyone. But don't you think with just a little more care your letters could look a little neater?"

❦

When we are trying to convince someone to do something or buy something, let's think continually of the advantage, to him, of doing as we wish. If the other person believes that he will gain little advantage from buying our product or from doing what we wish him to do, he will have little inclination to do as we desire. Sell products and ideas by concentrating on the advantages to the buyer. Selling becomes automatic when we concentrate on working for the other man's best interests.

❦

When we learn that someone has spread malicious gossip about us, we should avoid being prodded into anger. Let's say, "Jim's a smart fellow. He's usually right." When we hear of someone attempting to list some of our bad mistakes we might reply, "He does not know me very well or he would have made a much longer list!" When our statement gets back to its originator it will put a stop to the gossip and we will have gained a friend.

❦

Frequently we need the approval of someone to get one of our ideas accepted or we need his help in some project. The best way to win the other person's support is to make him a part of the idea or project. Make him feel that *our* problem is *his* problem. Try asking, not for his approval, but rather, "How can I proceed to get my idea accepted?" Or ask, "What would you do if you were I?" Or perhaps ask, "May I have your ideas on solving this problem?"

If you are a salesman trying to sell steel shelving to the purchasing agent of a chain of food stores, don't just ask him for an order. Rather ask, "How can I go about convincing food stores of the advantages of *steel* over wood shelving?" He will try to think hard of why steel is superior to wood shelving and thereby sell himself.

Ask the other man to participate in the idea or project or problem. Make him part of the plan by asking for his advice or his opinion. That is the easy way to achieve our objectives and gain the cooperation of those who can help us.

When trying to convince others to do as we desire it is most effective to use words that assume they will cooperate. Let's not ask, "Will you do this?" but rather say, "When you do this . . ."

No one likes to feel that we are influencing him. Everyone desires to make decisions of his own. To influence another to come around to our way of thinking, let's simply introduce a mild suggestion. We might use such phrases as "What do you think of . . ." or "I'm sure you've thought of this, but . . ." or "Is there any possibility of this working?" or "Is there any merit to trying an entirely different angle?" or "Do you think we ought to consider the possibility of . . ." A very direct suggestion preceded by the expression "As you know," as long as you are stating something the other person might conceivably know (*and don't* use that expression otherwise!), can readily permit your listener to treat the idea as his own.

As the suggestion begins to percolate in his mind, he will begin to arrive at our way of thinking. When he does, he will firmly believe it is his own idea! And, believing it is his own idea, he will easily work up enough enthusiasm to put it into operation! Our own objective is thus accomplished. *The mild suggestion is the great catalyst in mental chemistry. Through suggestion all things can be achieved.*

❦❦

When we are selling products and ideas, let's forget about selling and concentrate on rendering a service. No one can resist us if we are trying to help him solve one of his problems.

❦❦

Ask questions! They win people to your way of thinking.

❦❦

Salesmen who keep trying to sell *things* would find things sell themselves if they would work at selling *themselves* first.

❦❦

If I tell a man that he is wrong I arouse his anger and as he spouts forth a stream of words to defend his position he becomes even more convinced of his correctness. If, on the other hand, I tell him I'm sorry but I don't understand his view and I ask him to explain further, then there is a good probability that he will, through his own words, convince himself of his error.

❦❦

To achieve *your* objective show the other person how he can achieve *his* objective.

10

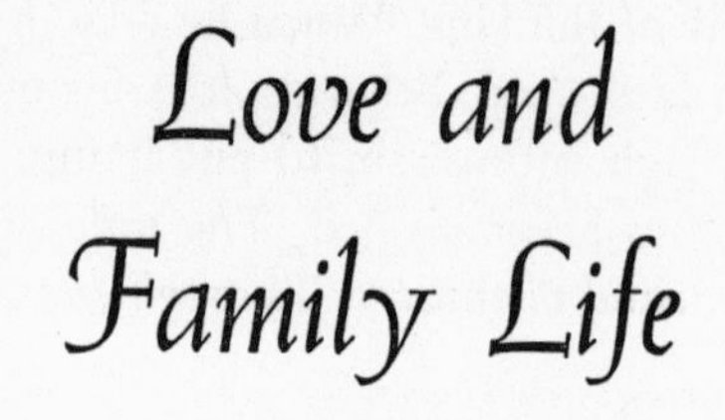

Love and Family Life

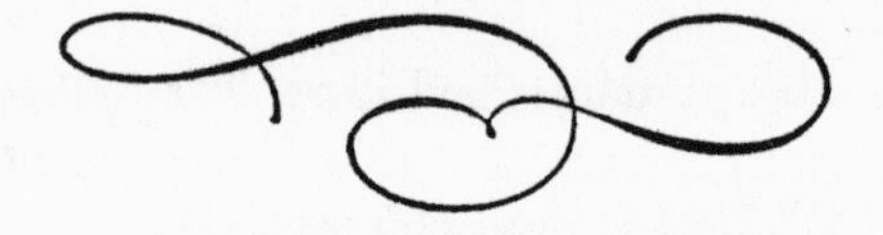

. . . *in spite of the deep-seated craving for love, almost everything else is considered to be more important than love: success, prestige, money, power—almost all our energy is used for the learning of how to achieve these aims, and almost none to learn the art of loving.*

—Erich Fromm

Infantile love follows the principle: "I love because I am loved." *Mature love follows the principle:* "I am loved because I love." *Immature love says:* "I love you because I need you." *Mature love says:* "I need you because I love you."

—Erich Fromm

. . . while one is consciously afraid of not being loved, the real, though usually unconscious fear is that of loving. *To love means to commit oneself without guarantee, to give oneself completely in the hope that our love will produce love in the loved person. Love is an act of faith, and whoever is of little faith is also of little love.*

—Erich Fromm

Love is not a natural phenomenon. Passion is. Selfishness is. But love is something that must be cultivated.

—Robert E. Moore

Children need models more than they need critics.

—Joseph Joubert

A *happy family is but an earlier heaven.*

—Sir John Bowring

The ability to say no is perhaps the greatest gift a parent has.

—Sam Levenson

God could not be everywhere, and therefore he created mothers.

—Jewish proverb

The heart has reasons that reason does not understand.

—Jacques Benigne Bossuet

There is a woman at the beginning of all great things.

—Alphonse de Lamartine

And though I have the gift of prophecy, and understand all mysteries, and all knowledge; and though I have all faith, so that I could remove mountains, and have not love, I am nothing.

—Apostle Paul (I Corinthians 13:2)

Love all God's creation, the whole and every grain of sand in it. Love every leaf, every ray of God's light. Love the animals, love the plants, love everything. If you love everything you will perceive the divine mystery in things. Once you perceive it, you will begin to comprehend it better every day. And you will come at last to love the whole world with an all-embracing love.

—Fëdor Dostoevski

Love is friendship set to music.

—CHANNING POLLOCK

If there is righteousness in the heart there will be beauty in the character. If there be beauty in the character, there will be harmony in the home. If there is harmony in the home, there will be order in the nation. When there is order in the nation, there will be peace in the world.

—CHINESE PROVERB

Love is the chrysalis of our happiness.

❦❦

Never treat the worst those whom you love the best.

❦❦

Love should be not only a reaction to love but a reaction to every other human action including those of impatience, unreasonableness, unkindness, bitterness, intolerance, and hate. Our love may wear the cloak of patience, of tolerance, or of firmness but even though it wears such a disguise is it therefore anything less than *love?*

❦❦

Is a mind filled with knowledge a more worthy objective than a heart full of love?

❦❦

Build in the child a love of knowledge and his store of facts will take care of itself.

❦❦

He who honors his father and mother is likely to be honored by his son and daughter.

❦❦

What are the two great needs of each of us? Someone to love us—someone for us to love.

❦❦

Have I done anything or said anything *today* that will make my wife feel that I love her and that I would be delighted to marry her again?

❦❦

Wouldn't the world be a happier place if those of us who are parents would realize that children misbehave when they feel threatened and insecure and unloved? It is when our children are acting their naughtiest that they need our love the most.

❦❦

To insure a happy marriage a man must not only pick the right wife but he must live in such a way that he convinces his wife that she has picked the right husband.

❦❦

Many parents believe that they should receive much of the credit for what their children are. Those parents should also realize that their own parents, in turn, deserve the credit for whatever they themselves are. Honor thy father and thy mother . . .

❦

After complimenting your child for a job well done, inspire him to even greater achievement by saying sincerely, *"I'm proud of you."*

❦

If enough "noes" and "can'ts" are said to a child, isn't it reasonable to believe that when he becomes an adult he will possess a well-trained subconscious that tells him not to try?

❦

A child must be made to realize, and be continually reminded of the fact, that his parents love him even during those times when they are punishing him. Children, like the rest of us, have an enormous appetite for love and appreciation.

❦

Parents of a naughty child might ask themselves whether the child's misbehavior is due to environment or heredity. If blame is reflexive isn't patience a greater virtue than naughtiness a vice?

❦

Some of the world's marriages might be saved if the wife and husband would never relate any troubles to the other until each has been well fed and is rested and relaxed.

❦

If we want a child to stop doing something, ask him to give us some good reasons why he shouldn't do that thing. If he cannot think of some good reasons let's send him to his room and allow him to return only after he has thought of some good reasons. The exercise will give the child some real understanding and perhaps make a sufficient impression on him so that he will refrain from such action in the future.

❧❧

Parents who are proud of the success they have achieved in spite of obstacles should not deprive their children of all of those same obstacles. The child showered with too many "advantages" may never know the satisfaction of having built a successful life through the overcoming of problems. Happiness results from the solving of problems, not through being presented with solutions.

❧❧

Here is a key to a happy marriage: Believe that your wife or your husband is the most important person in the world and demonstrate that belief by frequent expressions of love.

❧❧

The love we give to our children is passed on by them to their children and then, in turn, to their children's children.

❧❧

We ought to be as courteous to the members of our immediate family as we would be to strangers. Virtually all the insulting things that are said, are said to loved ones—wives, husbands, children—to those who will forgive even when treated meanly. Give a smile instead of a snarl, appreciation instead of criticism. Let's treat our loved ones as if they were strangers—better yet, as if they were friends.

❧❧

There will be better children when there are better parents.

Let's never let a day end with our being angry at someone we love. We can say, "I'm sorry. It's my fault that we don't agree. Even if I can't see it your way, I love you."

The measure of our poverty or of our wealth is the love we give and the love we receive.

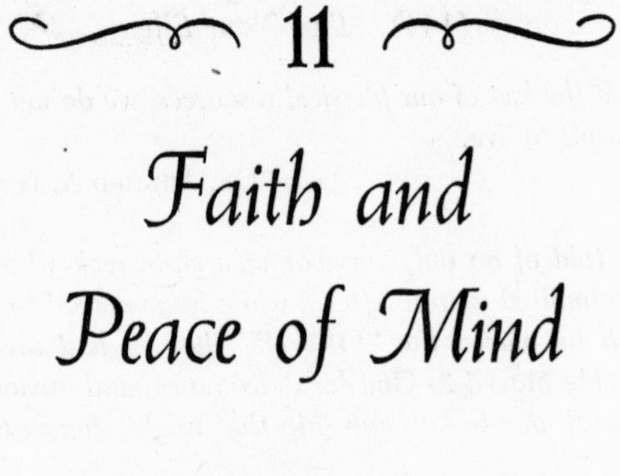

11 Faith and Peace of Mind

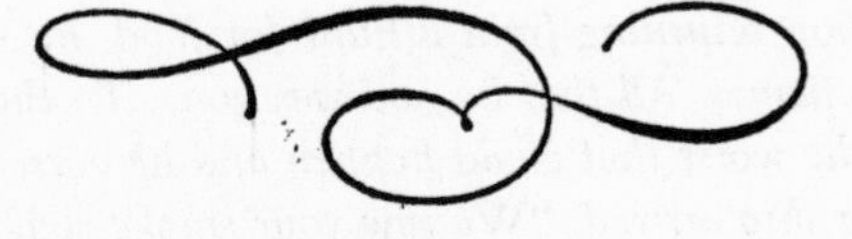

People forget that leisure is a form of prayer; that when we lie on the beach, relax in the hammock, close a book on our finger for a moment of thought, or even pause in the toil of the day for a breath and a sigh, we have moved for a moment in secret into the realm of prayer to ask for meaning.

—Robert Raynolds

To plow is to pray—to plant is to prophesy, and the harvest answers and fulfills.

—Robert G. Ingersoll

We die only when we are ready to die. We die when we want to die. We die because unconsciously we want to die, although consciously we may believe that we have everything to live for.

If we truly wish to live, if we have the incentive to live, if we have something to live for—*then no matter how sick we may be, if we have not exhausted the last of our physical resources, we do not die. We live* because *we want to live.*

—Dr. Arnold A. Hutschnecker

The story is told of an only survivor of a shipwreck who was thrown upon an uninhabited island. After a while he managed to build a rude hut in which he placed the "little all" that he had saved from the sinking ship. He prayed to God for deliverance, and anxiously scanned the horizon each day to hail any ship that might chance to be passing that way.

One day, upon returning from a hunt for food, he was horrified to find his hut in flames. All that he had was gone. To the man's limited vision, it was the worst that could happen and he cursed God. Yet the very next day a ship arrived. "We saw your smoke signal," the captain said.

—*Guideposts* (July, 1956)
Adapted from *Better Church Bulletins* by Stella O. Barnett

He prayeth best who loveth best
All things both great and small . . .
—Samuel T. Coleridge

The most beautiful thing we can experience is the mysterious. It is the source of all true art and science. He to whom this emotion is a stranger, who can no longer pause to wonder and stand rapt in awe, is as good as dead; his eyes are closed. . . . To know that what is impenetrable to us really exists, manifesting itself as the highest wisdom and the most radiant beauty which our dull faculties can comprehend only in their most primitive forms—this knowledge, this feeling, is at the center of true religiousness. In this sense, and in this sense only, I belong in the ranks of devoutly religious men.

—Albert Einstein

If one sets aside time for a business appointment, a trip to the hairdresser, a social engagement, or a shopping expedition, that time is accepted as inviolable. But if one says: I cannot come because that is my hour to be alone, one is considered rude, egotistical or strange. What a commentary on our civilization, when being alone is considered suspect; when one has to apologize for it, make excuses, hide the fact that one practices it—like a secret vice!

Actually these are among the most important times in one's life—when one is alone. Certain springs are tapped only when we are alone.

—Anne Morrow Lindbergh

The materialist is like a man who should explain the Ninth Symphony by faithfully tracing the pedigree of the catgut in the violins, but omitting to mention the unseen composer, whose mind speaks to us through those instruments.

—Alfred Noyes

There are more things in heaven and earth, Horatio,
Than are dreamt of in your philosophy.

—William Shakespeare

The only religion that will do anything toward enriching your life is the religion which inspires you to do something toward enriching the life of others.

—Unknown

The true test of a man's worth is not his theology but his life.

—The Talmud

Time is the image of eternity.

—Plato (Quoted by Diogenes Laërtius)

Some beliefs are rigid, like the body of death, impotent in a changing world. Other beliefs are pliable, like the young sapling, ever growing with the upward thrust of life.

—Sophia Lyon Fahs

The mystery of life is not a problem to be solved, but a reality to be experienced.

—UNKNOWN

There are things we know but cannot tell.

—MICHAEL POLANYI

The most learned of the microbes that live beneath my fingernail does not believe in the existence of me, of skyscrapers, of Paris, or of the stars. It is quite as possible to believe too little as it is to believe too much.

Why should one regret the passing of his youth? Only the decades can bring the happiness which comes with the realization that a concern for others transcends an interest in oneself.

Believe in the possibility of the impossible! I am not asking that you believe that 3 plus 4 equals 5 but merely in the possibility that 3 plus 4 *could* equal 5 (as can, in fact, be true in the case of vectors). Learn to believe! *Believe in the possibility of the impossible!*

A *prayer:* We ask for others all the good things we might like to ask for ourselves.

Success is a question of definition. Our definition ought to include a reference to peace of mind. Success involves not only material but spiritual satisfaction in the life we live.

No science can ever give an exact picture of the universe—of any of its parts or of any of its processes. Science continually strives, however, for more exact statements of the operations of nature. Science is a key for unlocking nature's secrets, but the door has an infinite number of locks. Perfection in the understanding of the laws of nature is an impossible goal. *Science* is the name we call the struggle to achieve that goal.

I have looked at God. I have seen the stars—and the face of a sleeping child.

I pray that I may act this fact: *A kindness is worth a thousand prayers.*

Perhaps religious people, world-wide, might be grouped into two sections—those who stress acts of belief and those who stress acts of service to others. Among the first group are those whose words and acts tend to keep men apart; among the second group are those whose actions are aimed toward producing a world united in friendship and love.

❧❧

I do not desire daily bread for me or for us alone but for all. I do not desire that my or our trespasses alone be forgiven but that everyone's trespasses be forgiven. I do not desire that I or we alone be not led into evil but that everyone be rightly directed. I do not desire that I or we alone should be free of pain and disease but that everyone should be free. I do not desire that I or we alone should be happy but that all should know happiness.

How many prayers have you or I said that are devoid of all selfishness? Suppose we were to set ourselves the project of composing such a prayer. Perhaps we might say:

> May all good things come to all living things in this and other worlds, in this and other galaxies. May I do my part this day and every day to help bring this about.

❧❧

Death is life's greatest experiment, life's greatest journey. Our great scientists, our great world travelers know less of this great experiment—this great journey—than even the least talented of those who have already embarked into the great unknown. We who see the beauty of the flaming sunset do not dread the night. There will be the splendor of a million stars!

❧❧

In the jungle of Tanganyika roams a huge elephant. On the skin of this elephant lives a tiny flea who studies his universe from tail to trunk, from back to foot. He is an authority on his universe and he lets his fellow fleas know it.

On this same elephant there is another flea who also knows this elephant universe quite thoroughly. But flea number two is a prophet who postulates the existence of other elephants, of other animals, of other lands and of a great flea god called man.

Can flea number two be right? Are there other elephants? Is there a flea god called man? Are there skyscrapers in New York?

What does man know of knowledge? What does a grain of sand know about a distant beach? What does the water dripping from a faucet know about the Baltic Sea?

12

Work, Ideas, and Problem Solving

I keep six honest serving men,
(They taught me all I knew)
Their names are What and Why and When
And How and Where and Who.

—Rudyard Kipling

When the public cannot understand a picture or a poem, they conclude that it is a bad picture or a bad poem. When they cannot understand the theory of relativity they conclude (rightly) that their education has been insufficient.

—Bertrand Russell

Genius for the most part is the brave use of past experience.

—James T. Mangan

Then felt I like some watcher of the skies
When a new planet swims into his ken;
Or like stout Cortez when with eagle eyes

He star'd at the Pacific—and all his men
Look'd at each other with a wild surmise—
Silent, upon a peak in Darien.

—John Keats

A Man's Mind may be likened to a garden, which may be intelligently cultivated or allowed to run wild; but whether cultivated or neglected, it must, and will, bring forth. *If no useful seeds are* put *into it then an abundance of useless weed-seeds will* fall *therein, and will continue to produce their kind.*

Just as a gardener cultivates his plot, keeping it free from weeds, and growing the flowers and fruits which he requires, so may a man tend the garden of his mind, weeding out all the wrong, useless, and impure thoughts, and cultivating toward perfection the flowers and fruits of right, useful, and pure thoughts. By pursuing this process, a man sooner or later discovers that he is the master-gardener of his soul, the director of his life. He also reveals, within himself, the laws of thought, and understands, with ever-increasing accuracy, how the thought-forces and mind-elements operate in the shaping of his character, circumstances, and destiny.

—James Allen

Don't be afraid to take a big step if one is indicated. You can't cross a chasm in two small jumps.

—David Lloyd George

Genius is one per cent inspiration and ninety-nine per cent perspiration.

—Thomas A. Edison

All history teaches us that these questions that we think the pressing ones will be transmuted before they are answered, that they will be replaced by others, and that the very process of discovery will shatter the concepts that we today use to describe our puzzlement.

—J. Robert Oppenheimer

Seven men went through a field, one after another. One was a farmer, he saw only the grass; the next was an astronomer, he saw the horizon and the stars; the physician noticed the standing water and suspected miasma; he was followed by a soldier, who glanced over the ground, found it easy to hold, and saw in a moment how the troops could be disposed; then came the geologist, who noticed the boulders and the sandy loam; after him came the real-estate broker, who bethought him how the line of the house lots should run, where would be the drive-way, and the stables. The poet admired the shadows cast by some trees, and still more the music of some thrushes and a meadow lark.

—RALPH WALDO EMERSON

Genius finds its own road, and carries its own lamp.

—ROBERT ARIS WILLMOTT

I do not know what I may appear to the world; but to myself I seem to have been only like a boy playing on the seashore, and diverting my-self in now and then finding a smoother pebble or a prettier shell than ordinary, whilst the great ocean of truth lay all undiscovered before me.

—SIR ISAAC NEWTON

Lost, somewhere between sunrise and sunset, sixty golden minutes. Each set with sixty diamond seconds. No reward is offered, for they are gone forever.

—HORACE MANN

Wisdom is *the principal thing;* therefore *get wisdom; and with all thy getting get understanding.*

—SOLOMON (Proverbs 4:7)

Man's capacities have never been measured. Nor are we to judge of what he can do by any precedents, so little has been tried.

—HENRY DAVID THOREAU

It is better to light one small candle than to curse the darkness.

—CONFUCIUS

Thank God every morning when you get up that you have something to do that day which must be done, whether you like it or not. Being forced to work and forced to do your best will breed in you temperance and self-control, diligence and strength of will, cheerfulness and content, and a hundred virtues which the idle never know.

—CHARLES KINGSLEY

If a man does not keep pace with his companions, perhaps it is because he hears a different drummer. Let him step to the music which he hears, however measured or far away.

—HENRY DAVID THOREAU

Common sense, do what it will, cannot avoid being surprised occasionally. The object of science is to spare it this emotion and create mental habits which shall be in such close accord with the habits of the world as to secure that nothing shall be unexpected.

—BERTRAND RUSSELL

The man who follows the crowd will never be followed by a crowd.

—DONNELL

Whenever you look at a piece of work and you think the fellow was crazy, then you want to pay some attention to that. One of you is likely to be, and you had better find out which one it is. It makes an awful lot of difference.

—CHARLES F. KETTERING

Read every day something no one else is reading. Think every day something no one else is thinking. It is bad for the mind to be always a part of a unanimity.

—CHRISTOPHER MORLEY

If you have advanced ideas on any subject, do not expect popular applause. The people seldom approve the pioneer. You must get your joy not from the cheers of the populace, but from self-expression. If your ideas are worth while and you have confidence in their value to the world, the approval of the multitude will be a matter of supreme indifference to you.

—THOMAS DREIER

The world fears a new experience more than it fears anything. Because a new experience displaces so many old experiences.

—D. H. LAWRENCE

No army can withstand the strength of an idea whose time has come.

—VICTOR HUGO

A scientist's originality lies in seeing a problem where others see none and finding a way to its pursuit where others lose their bearings.

—MICHAEL POLANYI

It is impossible to predict what is not possible.

Facts are the trees in wisdom's forest. Let's not fail to find the forest because we are concentrating on two or three trees.

Flowers of truth grow on Superstition Mountain.

Facts are probabilities which we trust until new data arrive. Let's be careful in dealing with others to avoid implying that we have cornered even an insignificant part of the truth market.

A little knowledge is always better than no knowledge. Not knowing how little is our knowledge is the dangerous thing.

❧❧

It is simple to make an easy job look like a hard one—just keep looking at it! It is simple to make a hard job look like an easy one—just do the work!

❧❧

If we are restless and find it difficult to fall alseep, let's put happy thoughts into our mind instead of putting pills into our stomach. We might ask ourselves, "What happy things have happened today?"

Did we see a flaming sunset—or smell a rose—or hear a child's laughter? Did we see icicles glistening in the sunlight—or do a good turn that wasn't discovered or one that was discovered by accident—or give a child a ride on a merry-go-round? If we are troubled with insomnia let's ask ourselves, "What happy things have happened today?"

❧❧

Each time we are faced with a decision it is meaningful to first decide if it is of minor or major importance. Shall we have eggs or pancakes for breakfast? Shall we take the boulevard or the toll road to the office? Let's decide such minor issues rapidly and without hesitation.

Perhaps our problem is more serious. And how do we decide whether or not it is serious? *We can ask ourselves if the consequences of our decision are apt to have any significance one year from today.* If they are not, let's make our decision rapidly. If the consequences of our decision are likely to have an important bearing on our future, we should collect all possible facts and data relating to the problem. Delay making a decision until all readily obtainable facts are known. *Then decide!*

Once our decision is made we should not waste time and energy worrying whether or not it was the correct one to make. Let's devote our time and energy to working hard at carrying out that decision toward the end of *making* it the correct one!

❦

In the matter of memory, good intention promotes good retention. If we intend to remember something or somebody, the chances are greatly increased that we will be able to do so.

Next time we are introduced to someone it will prove helpful if we tell ourselves, "I *must* remember this man." When we learn a new fact that we believe is important, we can tell ourselves, "I *must* remember this fact." Having told ourselves that we *must* remember, probabilities are that we *will* remember!

❦

Progress is achieved by assuming the attitude that nothing being done anywhere is being done in the best possible way.

❦

Energy is often wasted in attempting to find a solution to a problem. Energies would, in many cases, be better applied toward first finding the exact nature of the problem. Once a problem is clearly defined, its solution often becomes evident.

If we ask, "How can we stop students from cheating during examinations?" we have failed to recognize the basic problem. In real life situations we are not asked to perform with complete reliance on our memory, but we find that most progress is made when we share our information with others and they, in turn, share theirs with us. The real problem is, "How can we construct our tests so that they are more similar to problem situations we meet outside of school?" *Structuring the examination questions so that books may be consulted* might be the answer that was sought.

When the *exact nature* of a problem is stated its solution often becomes simple.

❧

Skepticism in regard to present methods and ideas can lead to progress. Skepticism can also result in a refusal to accept the new, the great, the untried.

❧

One technique for fighting procrastination is to convert our problem into visible form. The method consists of simply writing on a piece of paper a word or two representing the problem. Perhaps the words might be "income tax," "medical examination," "loan," "advertising schedule," or "change tires."

Next step is to put the paper right in the middle of the desk or breakfast table or some other place where it will constantly be in our way. Then we tell ourselves that the note will stay right there being a nuisance to us until we solve our problem. Because of our desire to get rid of this annoyance—this note which is constantly in our way—we gain the added incentive needed to work toward our problem's solution.

❧

How do we manufacture ideas? By taking a pencil and paper and starting to write or to doodle or to draw. Ideas will come.

❧

Knowledge is not power but represents potential power. Action—knowledge in motion—does the work of the world.

Only through the application of knowledge can we gain power. It is the *doing* rather than the *knowing* that leads us to success. The world cares little for the state of our knowledge; it grants rewards in proportion to what we *do* or can get others to do.

❧

Many persons have found that the subconscious mind solves their problems while they are in bed and their conscious mind is sleeping. It is a good idea to keep a pencil and pad of paper handy at the bedside to record these valuable ideas as soon as we awake from an idea-creating sleep. Let's write down those ideas immediately; to delay is to run the risk of losing them.

Where facts are scarce, men have a tendency to fill the void with opinions, beliefs, arguments, and mistakes. It is better to seek facts first and form opinions second. Later, when the facts change, let's be willing and unashamed to "change our minds."

If time is money shouldn't we spend time as carefully as we spend our money?

Failure to learn is never the fault of just the student whether the student is in a pupil-teacher, child-parent, or employee-boss relationship. Can the subject be made more interesting? Can the subject be related to something the student thinks *is* important?

We should beware of reasoning such as "You are either for me or against me," or "You must be for cows wearing red ribbons or against cows wearing red ribbons." It is possible that you just don't care what I do or what cows wear.

To write a sales letter, to write an article, or to write a book, accomplish your objective by starting to write! Put something on that piece of paper!

Suppose you plan to write a sales letter or a magazine article about milling cutters. Perhaps you might put these words on your paper:

It is said by some that the moon is made of green cheese. It might not be impossible to find some who might use green cheese in the manufacture of milling cutters.

Never mind how ridiculous or irrelevant these first words may be. The main thing now is to keep on writing. After a paragraph or two you will begin to make sense. When your work is finished, throw away the first paragraph or two and the job is done!

❦❦

Experience is the second best teacher. Shouldn't we be able to achieve through thought more of those things that we seem able to learn only through experience?

❦❦

Low-level conversation deals with persons; higher level conversation deals with events. Highest level conversation deals with a discussion of persons and of events only insofar as such discussion contributes to a formulation or elucidation of a principle, an idea, a hypothesis, or a theory.

❦❦

Asking a good question frequently requires more ingenuity than giving a good answer.

❦❦

How can one set out to construct an epigram? Let's start with a standard one:

An ounce of prevention is worth a pound of cure.

Then let's change it word by word through successive stages as follows:

1. An ounce of *silence* is worth a pound of *regret.*

And then,

2. An ounce of silence *can prevent* a pound of regret.
   And finally,
3. An *inch* of silence can prevent a *mile* of regret.

Thinking about the work has been known to make one more tired than doing the work itself.

When statistics can predict, why let luck decide?

One of the sure ways to fail in a difficult project is to demand that all steps to the goal be clearly delineated before you take step number one. Take the first step toward success. Proceed in faith that the second step will become apparent. It will!

"Sleeping on it" is one of the best techniques for problem solving. But don't sleep on it too long!

A mark of proficiency in problem-solving is knowing when one should stop trying to solve a problem by oneself and call in an expert to do the work.

In the words of Gilbert Murray, "The great difference, intellectually speaking, between one man and another is simply the number of things they can see in a given cubic yard of the world."

There are many "cubic yards" to challenge the intellectually alive person. Not only physical earth yards await our study but all the range of interests that men have had since they took their families to live in caves, up to the latest thoughts men have had this morning at 7:30. Would we like to be more alive intellectually? Here is a way! Let's make a list of subjects in which we feel we are very *ignorant*. Perhaps such a list might include the following:

horse racing
analyzing financial statements
trigonometry
commodity futures and
American poetry since 1930.

The important thing about compiling such a list is that we include no subject in which we feel even moderately competent. It should be a list of subjects about which we feel absolutely stupid.

What do we do with this list? We select one of the items, go to the library and scan or read everything we can on this topic. To wake up to life, to learn more about one of the world's "cubic yards," start now to use this method! Next week, Tuesday, we select topic number two.

❧❧

When a man looks upon a problem as an exciting safari into the unknown, at the end of that safari he will find success. A successful life consists of many daily successes in solving *problems* that were thought of as *challenges*. Welcome the next problem! Plan your next safari!

❧❧

If we tried to invest our time as carefully as we try to invest our money, we might have more of the money.

❧❧

A ton of superstition may yield an ounce of truth.

❦

One of the primary causes of mental stress is the frustration that results from an attempt to do "everything at once." The cure is to prepare a daily schedule of things to be done. List the day's projects in order of importance or in order of unpleasantness. Limit the list to the most important projects and include only enough items so that the total represents a reasonably possible program. Tackle the most important or the least pleasant jobs first and cross them off the list as they are completed. One after another, finish each item on that list, resisting the temptation to do things not on the list. Unfinished tasks induce tension, finished ones promote relaxation. The written schedule is a tool that insures our progress and promotes serenity.

❦

A powerful device for increasing our ability to solve problems rapidly is that of role-playing. We imagine ourselves to be confronted with various problems and work out in our minds the words we would say and the actions we would take. We consider various questions that we might be asked and then work out the answers we would give. Even if the problems when they eventuate are not quite as we imagined they might be, or if the questions we are asked differ from those we have rehearsed, our role-playing will still have been of great value. It will have given us greater confidence in meeting the problems and allow us to act more correctly and with greater spontaneity.

"Bridges" crossed "before you come to them" are often crossed more smoothly when you *actually* come to them.

❦

When a problem seems difficult allow the subconscious to take over while you fill your conscious mind with other matters.

Periodically, drag out the problem to see if your subconscious is ready to provide the answer. Don't worry or lose sleep over your problem; your subconscious will, sooner or later, give you the solution.

❧❧

What can we do about that stack of unread magazines, that shelf of unread books? Let's give ourselves fifteen minutes to read each magazine, an hour or two to read each book. We read the first two or three paragraphs and the last paragraph of any articles in the magazine that interest us and skip the others. (Incidentally, we handle the daily newspaper the same way except we read only the opening paragraphs.) Using this technique we completely read only those relatively few articles that are extremely interesting or may prove helpful in solving one of our problems. These are the articles that might provide help in some of our home, work or community projects, or might help improve our relations with others or with ourselves by providing relaxation, entertainment, or a fuller understanding of the world around us.

To dispose of nonfiction books we will read the opening and closing chapter plus a paragraph here and another there throughout the rest of the volume in order to get a general view of the subject being covered. Then we can put the book back on our shelf with the satisfaction of knowing exactly where to find information on this subject should the need arise. If we discover a book that contains material either especially interesting in itself or valuable for a project in which we are engaged, let's budget enough time to read it more thoroughly.

Works of fiction, as a group, need not average very many hours if we immediately stop reading any book after two or three chapters if the author has not succeeded in captivating us. Giving up the reading of an occasional work of fiction that has failed to make us interested and giving additional hours to those books we find interesting will get us through a stack of fiction books with just a few hours average reading time per volume.

When we call someone a criminal, a sinner, a bad boy or a failure we instill in him a feeling that he is helpless to prevent future wrong-doing or failure. The words are unfortunate; they imply an inevitable compulsion to perform acts in accordance with the name given the actor.

An idea is worthless until action brings it to fruition. Let's stop thinking and hoping long enough to ask ourselves, "What *action* is needed now?" And when we clearly see what action is needed, let's *act* on that revelation. When the proper action is not clearly indicated we should act anyway, correcting our errors as we go along. If we act as if nothing stands in our way, behold! nothing will stand in our way.

Physical posture is related to mental attitude:

1. We are happy because we smile.
2. We are creative because we ride to the office on different roads each morning and so get away from in-the-rut type of acting and thinking.
3. We relax because we wear casual clothes.
4. We can write (as many authors have discovered) if we will just start to write anything (even though we may throw away the first few sentences). If we just start writing, soon we'll write acceptable material.

Let's assume the physical posture that will lead to happy, creative and otherwise good consequences.

❦❦

The time we spend on our job *beyond* the eight hour day can be made to pay off, in general, at a rate far in excess of our hourly wage. Working on the special project requiring time that is hard to find in the regular working day, reading about our job or profession, designing a new work-flow, planning for a speech that can further our professional status—these are activities that often lead to a big pay-off.

❦❦

Completion of a big project is achieved through first breaking it down into separate small projects and then, in turn, completing each of them.

❦❦

Make a note of it! The most disorganized persons are those who have an inflated idea of the quality of their memory.

❦❦

Those who complain of not having enough time to do the things they would like to do often are victims of the inability to say "No." When requested to run for office or to join committees they frequently agree without asking themselves if such an activity contributes importantly to the objective of promoting themselves or is in the mainstream of their own chosen channel for serving mankind. If "no" is the answer they give to their self-asked question, then "no" should be their prompt answer to the job being offered. If "yes" is the answer to their self-asked question, then let them say "yes!" to the offer and promptly immerse themselves in the project with unbounded enthusiasm!

Wisdom consists—not so much of having the answers—but of asking appropriate questions and then searching for the answers.

Any statement that contains one or more of the words that are trademarks of the sweeping generalization has a high probability of being false. Some of these words are: *all, always, every, everyone, no one, none, never, can't, impossible, forever, invariably, totally, wholly, completely,* and *absolutely.*

The biggest pay-offs are not made in accordance with the hours put in on the job but for the quality and quantity of creative ideas that are put into action.

How do we end our procrastination and make a decision? Good decisions are made by following a logical analysis such as the following and *outlining on a piece of paper considerations under each of these five points:*

1. *What is the problem? What are we attempting to do?* It is vital to arrive at a clear statement of the problem and of our objective rather than leave it in the hazy realm of the indefinite.
2. *What are the facts relating to this problem? What factors seem to be the cause of the problem? When do they occur?* Try to gain as much information as possible about the problem through books, interviews, analysis of available data, and so forth.
3. *What are all possible ways of solving this problem?* Do not jump to the conclusion that there is only one way of han-

dling the problem. Write down all possible answers to this question.

4. *Which course of action will provide the best answer to this problem?* Be sure we consider various alternatives. The most direct course of action may not necessarily provide the greatest satisfaction and happiness.
5. *When are we going to take action?* In some cases a proper analysis of all factors will indicate delay is advisable. Perhaps new information will be available next Tuesday which may make possible a better choice of decisions. But watch out! Here is where the negative and positive thinkers are separated. The negative thinker will continually dream up reasons why his decision, already arrived at, should not be put into effect. The positive thinker, unless he comes up with a good reason to delay, puts his decision into effect *immediately*. The doers, those who do the world's work, those who worry least, those who are happiest, have a policy of *doing it now!*

Let's use this technique to identify a problem clearly, to discover the causes of the problem, to develop all possible solutions and, having done this, to obtain the best possible solution and to decide on a course of action. Here is a procedure we can employ regularly to reduce worry about our problems and to arrive at sensible solutions.

❦❦

A child represents *enthusiasm personified*. Everything delights him—a flower, mommy's pots and pans, a light bulb, a new dog that has just moved into the neighborhood or one of the old dogs. He studies each object, bites it, bangs on it, takes it apart. The child is curious. He is alive!

When did we lose our curiosity? Chances are we *have* lost most of that constantly inquiring spirit of the child. But need it be lost forever? Why not promise ourselves we will once again become curious and thus start again to live life sensitively and more fully? Count the petals on a flower; check the time between the lightning's flash and the sound of thunder; determine, on days of different temperature, the number of chirps per minute made by a cricket.

Let's resolve to become as little children by permitting our curiosity to make us alive. *Curiosity is the secret of perpetual youth!*

❧

Use Ben Franklin's method for aid in solving a problem and for deciding on a course of action. This is a technique based on the idea that it is difficult to keep in mind, simultaneously, all the points favoring and those against taking a certain action. We may on occasion choose a particular course of action. A few moments later, after recalling facts opposing such a procedure, we may decide to act quite differently. Here is Franklin's method for solving this dilemma.

Take a piece of paper and, by drawing a vertical line down the middle, produce two columns. Write "Pro" over one of the columns and "Con" over the other. Then record in the proper column short hints regarding reasons for or against the proposed idea or action. After the two lists seem complete attempt to weigh the relative importance of the various entries. If we find a "pro" reason that seems equal to one of the "con" reasons strike them both out. If we find two "pro" reasons that seem equal to three "con" reasons strike out all five accordingly. Using such a procedure it is easy to determine whether the bulk of the evidence is in favor of, or is opposed to, the idea or action being analyzed.

This is what Franklin called "moral or prudential algebra"—a mathematics that we should find applicable to many of life's problems.

❧❧

Devote a few minutes each evening to an analysis of our activities of that day. What did we accomplish? What was left undone? What will we do tomorrow?

❧❧

After another of many, many failures in attempting to find a satisfactory filament for his yet-to-be-invented incandescent lamp, Edison said, "Now we know another thing that won't work. That's progress."

Let's welcome failures. When we have a complete catalog of all the methods, materials, or ideas that will not work we'll also have what we're looking for—the one that *will*.

❧❧

Problems sometimes are solved by our subconscious mind. When we find it impossible to resolve a problem we might try escaping from it a while. Let's go to a movie, play tennis, read a book, or take a bus ride. Then return to the problem. Frequently the solution will then be apparent and a course of action will be obvious.

❧❧

The first step in learning any subject or skill is to tell ourselves that we haven't tried instead of saying that we can't. We should not tell ourselves "I can't ice skate" or "I can't read the stock market reports in the daily newspapers" when we mean we haven't *tried*. Demosthenes, who stuttered as a child, became the greatest orator of ancient Athens. Let's not say we *can't* when we mean we haven't *tried*.

Let's develop our prejudices to fit our reasons, not our reasons to fit our prejudices.

A primary purpose of education should be, not that we learn only theory and fact, but rather that we learn to love learning.

In learning how to make enough money to give us leisure, and in acting on that knowledge, we should not fail to learn how to use the leisure we will eventually achieve.

It is often a mistake to disclose a new idea to others before it is fully developed. At its birth a new idea is seldom strong enough to withstand any negative criticism. Let's conserve the energy we would expend in telling others about our plans and use that energy for their development. When our idea has finally taken shape it will be strong enough to withstand the negative criticism to which new ideas are generally subjected. Then, too, if plans are disclosed to others too soon, we tend to do, not necessarily what we think we should, but what those who have heard our plans will expect us to do. Plans kept secret can be modified, or completely dropped without embarrassment.

There is learning to be found not only in the studying of an encyclopedia but in the reading of a poem, in the viewing of a painting, in the smelling of a rose, in the listening to the song of a bird, in the enjoyment of a sunset, and in the experiencing of the smile of a man.

Make up a list of inspirational words that you associate with each initial of your name—and therefore with yourself. Commit to memory and periodically review when in need of inspiration. The following is an example that might serve as a guide in constructing a similar list for yourself:

W Work and Will.
A Attitude. (I assume the attitude that nothing short of full success is satisfactory or even possible.)
L Love. (Love makes the world—and me—go 'round.)
T Try!
E Energy.
R Reasoning.

A Attention and Action. (I pay attention. I listen and I look. I not only think, I *act!*)
L Live Life!
B Brave *or* Bluff. (I will be brave or I will bluff.)
E Enjoy! (I enjoy every moment of my life!)
R Relax. (I will work while I work and play while I play, and then completely relax.)
T Time. (Every hour has sixty minutes to be used rather than abused or neglected.)

H Help and Hope. (Help others. Hope, and work to make that hoping come true.)
E Enthusiasm.
I Interest and Inspiration. (I am interested in all that is human. I will try to inspire others.)
B Boylike. (Boylike, I retain the enthusiasm, the energy, the curiosity of my boyhood.)
Y Yes! (I say "Yes!" to life.)